Praise for
He Calls You Beautiful

"Dee Brestin has a lovely, lyrical writing voice, perfectly suited to the Song of Songs. Verse by verse, she engages each of our five senses to help us truly experience the breathtaking love of God. The resources and questions she offers for Bible studies are exceptional. And her sheer passion for Him captures our hearts and minds until we too are swept up in His divine dance. *He Calls You Beautiful* is just that— *beautiful*. I learned so much and loved every word!"

> —LIZ CURTIS HIGGS, best-selling author
> of *31 Verses to Write on Your Heart*

"Every woman's heart longs for her own personal love story in which she is desired, pursued, and cherished. As I read Dee's new book, *He Calls You Beautiful*, I wept again and again at the depth of love God has for me and for you. I underlined whole paragraphs so I could go back and read them again. If you long for your faith to move out of your head and into your heart, savor this book. You will feel undeniably loved."

> —LESLIE VERNICK, Christian counselor, relationship
> coach, speaker, and author of numerous books including
> *The Emotionally Destructive Marriage*

"Dee Brestin joyfully leads readers through the enigmatic book of Song of Songs, causing our hearts to melt with the beauty of Christ and making us long for more intimacy with Christ."

> —NANCY GUTHRIE, author of the Seeing Jesus
> in the Old Testament Bible study series

"Bernard of Clairvaux, one of the most beloved and influential writers of the Middle Ages, believed he could interpret the entire Bible through one book, the Song of Songs. Imagine seeing not the Gospels or Galatians or Romans but the Song of Songs as the best lens for understanding all of God's heart in all of God's Word. This seems strange to those of us who might approach this book of the Bible with detached curiosity and lingering questions. Yet drawing on trusted resources and relentlessly pointing her readers back to communion with Christ, Dee Brestin similarly navigates between the false choices of romantic love poem or simple allegory to help readers embrace the modern-day relevance of this ancient song."

—RANKIN WILBOURNE, pastor and author of *Union with Christ*

"In *He Calls You Beautiful,* Dee Brestin poignantly weaves together story and biblical truths to illustrate God's enraptured heart for His people. Several times as I read these pages, it was almost as if His breath was on the back of my neck. I had chills, feeling this nearness that Dee extracts so aptly from the Song of Songs. Just one chapter into this book and I was already making a list of friends with whom to share it. This is an excellent read for the hungry believer."

—SARA HAGERTY, author of *Every Bitter Thing Is Sweet*

"Dee Brestin's fine books always strike me as deeply human, *personal* in the very best sense. This one is supremely so. Dee has done her homework. Taking the Song of Songs as a living picture of an intimate relationship with the Lord Jesus, she traces the relationship from before its beginning to its death-defeating end. Even those Bible students who do not follow all the parallels she sees will be greatly enriched by letting her help them dig into this Old Testament illustration of Christ and His bride, the church."

—GREG R. SCHARF, professor of homiletics and chair
of the department of pastoral theology, Trinity Evangelical
Divinity School, and author of *Relational Preaching:
Knowing God, His Word, and Your Hearers*

"My years of ministry to women struggling with relational and sexual brokenness have shown me how often they find it difficult to understand the depths of Jesus's tender love for us and how He actually can transform our lives! People all around us have distorted views of sexuality and feel trapped in patterns of disordered desires. Now in *He Calls You Beautiful,* I have a resource to offer that plumbs the beauty and wonder of intimate love with God, and the glory of His design for sexuality within marriage. I highly commend this book to the single and married, younger and older, because it will guide you through the Song of Solomon, a book often misunderstood or avoided, into the spacious place of intimacy with Christ!"

—ELLEN MARY DYKAS, women's ministry director
at Harvest USA and author of *Sexual Sanity for Women*

HE CALLS
YOU
Beautiful

BOOKS BY DEE BRESTIN

The Friendships of Women

Idol Lies

The God of All Comfort

Falling in Love with Jesus (coauthored with Kathy Troccoli)

DEE'S BIBLE STUDIES SERIES

A Woman of Wisdom

A Woman of Worship

A Woman of Contentment

A Woman of Love

A Woman of Beauty

FISHERMAN BIBLE STUDYGUIDES

Examining the Claims of Jesus

Proverbs and Parables

Building Your House on the Lord

Friendship

A full list of Dee's books can be found on her website: DeeBrestin.com

HE CALLS YOU *Beautiful*

HEARING *the* VOICE *of* JESUS *in the* SONG *of* SONGS

DEE BRESTIN

Best-selling author of *The Friendships of Women*

MULTNOMAH

HE CALLS YOU BEAUTIFUL

All Scripture quotations, unless otherwise indicated, are taken from the ESV® Bible (the Holy Bible, English Standard Version®), ESV® Permanent Text Edition® (2016), copyright © 2001 by Crossway, a publishing ministry of Good News Publishers. Used by permission. All rights reserved. Scripture quotations marked (KJV) are taken from the King James Version. Scripture quotations marked (NIV) are taken from the Holy Bible, New International Version®, NIV®. Copyright © 1973, 1978, 1984 by Biblica Inc.® Used by permission. All rights reserved worldwide. Scripture quotations marked (NRSV) are taken from the New Revised Standard Version Bible, copyright © 1989, Division of Christian Education of the National Council of the Churches of Christ in the United States of America. Used by permission. All rights reserved.

Italics in Scripture quotations reflect the author's added emphasis.

Details in some anecdotes and stories have been changed to protect the identities of the persons involved.

Trade Paperback ISBN 978-1-60142-990-2
eBook ISBN 978-1-60142-991-9

Copyright © 2017 by Dee Brestin

Cover design by Kelly L. Howard; cover photography by KNSY

Published in the United States by Multnomah, an imprint of the Crown Publishing Group, a division of Penguin Random House LLC, New York.

MULTNOMAH® and its mountain colophon are registered trademarks of Penguin Random House LLC.

The Cataloging-in-Publication Data is on file with the Library of Congress.

2017—First Edition

147028622

Dedicated to Linda Strom.

How radiant you are as you look to Him,
"beautiful as the moon, bright as the sun."
You and your vast team of prison volunteers are
"awesome as an army with banners."
—*Song of Songs 6:10*

Except you enthrall me, never shall be free,
Nor ever chaste, except you ravish me.

**—John Donne, "Holy Sonnets: Batter My Heart,
Three-Person'd God"**

Contents

Invincible Love: IT IS WELL WITH MY SOUL

FACILITATOR RESOURCES

How to Use This Book

Welcome to what I pray will be a book that stirs your wonder at the depth of Christ's love for you.

Following each chapter of this book is a Bible study so that your small group (or you alone) can hear the voice of Jesus in the Song of Songs. It is one thing to read what I have to say about Jesus in the Song, but it is quite another to discover Him there yourself!

The Song of Songs is too rich a study for you to come to your small group unprepared. Because the Song is all about developing intimacy with the Lord, I encourage you to do a little reading and study each day so that you develop the habit of spending time with the One who calls to you, "Come away, my love."

To interest your friends in this study, you can e-mail them this link to a two-minute overview: www.deebrestin.com/hecallsyoubeautiful. (This link also has all the songs, videos, and mp3 sermons in case they won't work on the Internet.) Let your friends know this women's study is for both singles and marrieds, for you will be focusing on Jesus's love for His bride and her responsive love to Him.

If you are the small-group facilitator, be sure to look each week at the section at the back of this book designed especially to help you prepare to lead your group through the study. If your group has the books before your first gathering, simply assign the first chapter to read and the first lesson to complete before you meet. But if they are not able to get the books until the first meeting or if your group is new and needs to get acquainted, instead begin that first week with the Get-Acquainted Lesson at the back of the book. That can be done on the spot without the participants doing any preparation. Then for the following week, assign the first chapter and the first lesson.

I'm excited to think of you beginning this journey of experiencing God's love. How I pray His Spirit will help you hear and respond to your Beloved.

—Dee

Overture

Yes, Jesus Loves Me!

———————⁓———————

The Best Song of All

Why God Put a Love Story in the Heart of His Word

I am now utterly convinced that on Judgment Day, the Lord
Jesus is going to ask each of us one question, and only one
question: "Did you believe that I love you?"

—Brennan Manning

*W*omen's prisons are my favorite places to speak. There I see a thirst for God that I seldom see outside prison walls, at least in our wealthy Western world. In prisons I see parched hearts soaking up the truth of the Bible. I see *life* sprouting before my eyes—life where there has been *no* life. Flinty faces soften, tearless eyes moisten.

I always leave the prison amazed. The God of the Bible is still opening blind eyes and transforming hearts. He is still coming to the outsider, the one whom the world does not value.

In a women's prison near Milwaukee, Wisconsin, God took my breath away with something only He could orchestrate. Fifty of the women at this correctional institute had completed one of my video Bible studies. Now I was going to speak to them. When I walked in, they gave me a royal welcome: jumping, clapping, and cheering. I laughed—how I wished we were allowed to hug! There is no bond like the bond of Christ. The light we recognized in one another's eyes was the same light: the light of Jesus, the light that overcame our darkness.

I opened by asking these precious women to share ways Jesus had met them in the study they had just completed. One woman said, "I didn't want to come to this study, but my cellmate kept bugging me. I told her to shut up, because there was no way I'd be caught at a group of Holy Rollers. One day she tossed her copy of your book on my bunk and said, 'Just look at it. If you come and hate it, I promise I'll never bug you again.'" She paused, overcome with emotion. Then she looked up, whispering, "I'm so glad I came."

We all exchanged smiles of understanding. Her story was ours, too. Each of us had resisted God. But He had persisted, ambushing us with His love.

As I began the study I'd planned for that night, I did so with trepidation. As I had prepared for the gathering, I sensed that God wanted me to show them His love for them as revealed in the Song of Songs, one of the most misunderstood books of the Bible. But as I was driving to Milwaukee, I began to wonder if I had indeed heard from the Lord.

What am I doing presenting such a challenging book to them? I thought. *They'll go back to their cells and read this very passionate love story and think, What in the world? What is this doing in the Bible? What could this possibly have to do with God and me?*

Yet I knew how badly they needed this message. Many of these women in prison had never experienced earthly love, either from parents or husbands. A very high percentage of them had experienced horrific physical or sexual abuse. They also made choices that landed them in prison and filled them with shame. Even after they came to Christ, believing that He died to pay their debt in full, they struggled to hold on to the truth that they had been cleansed and were beautiful in His eyes.

And so I plunged ahead, pleading for God's Spirit to move. I asked them to open their Bibles to the Song of Songs, a small book in the Old Testament.

"This book has been captivating hearts for thousands of years," I told them. "Sometimes it's called 'The Song of Solomon.' But like 'King of kings' or 'Lord of lords,' the title 'Song of Songs' implies this song is the very best song of all. And what is that? It is always the love song of Jesus."

I told them that it was an earthly love story, a song of love between a man and a woman, but that it was intended to help them understand a much deeper love story: the love between Christ and His bride.

I explained, "God uses many metaphors in Scripture to show us that Christianity is not rules or ritual but relationship. The Lord compares Himself to a friend who is closer than a brother, to a father who cherishes his child, and finally, the most intimate metaphor of all, to a bridegroom who rejoices over his bride.

"When God brought Eve to Adam to be his wife, Adam erupted in praise, and God said, 'A man shall leave his father and his mother and hold fast to his wife, and they shall become one flesh' (Genesis 2:24). This excitement that Adam felt for Eve is the same joy God feels for His bride, for Isaiah tells us, 'As the bridegroom rejoices over the bride, so shall your God rejoice over you' (Isaiah 62:5)."

The women were listening intently. I saw both hope and doubt flicker across faces. *Could it be true?*

"This verse about a man leaving his father and mother and holding fast to his wife is repeated three more times in Scripture. It culminates in Ephesians when, after it appears the fourth time, a secret is revealed: 'A man shall leave his father and mother and hold fast to his wife, and the two shall become one flesh. This mystery is profound, and I am saying that it refers to Christ and the church' (Ephesians 5:31–32)."

The church, I explained, means the bride of Christ, true believers. The beauty of marriage as God intended it is meant to illuminate His mysterious relationship with us. "Your Maker," the Bible tells us, "is your husband" (Isaiah 54:5).

I knew some of these women would struggle with this picture, in the same way that some struggled with the picture of God as their Father. Just as many had been abused as children, many had been abused as wives. Instead of terms of endearment, they'd been called cruel names, "rash words," which Proverbs 12:18 says "are like sword thrusts." Instead of feeling cherished in the marriage bed, they'd felt used. Instead of knowing faithfulness, they'd experienced treachery as their husbands walked out on them and their young children. Instead of being encouraged to be the women God created them to be, they'd been drawn into addictions and crimes.

I looked at Lila, remembering her story. She'd told me earlier that though now her security was in Jesus, it used to be in her husband. She'd been the getaway driver for his bank robberies. Now they both had long prison sentences and their children were in foster care.

I took a deep breath and said, "I know this is hard for so many of you. Many of you have never been loved like this by an earthly husband. But a beautiful earthly marriage is possible in Christ, and that is the picture in the Song." I saw the longing in their eyes. "But even if God never gives you a godly husband or turns your husband into a godly man, you have a Bridegroom who absolutely cherishes you like the bridegroom in the Song."

"That's the truth," one woman said. "Jesus will never walk out on me."

I nodded. "That's right. *Never* will He leave you."

Then I gave them a thumbnail sketch of the Cinderella story of the Song. "A great shepherd-king falls in love with a peasant girl who works in one of his vineyards. He chooses her, loves her, leads her through the wilderness, and goes away, but he will come back for her. She is transformed in this story because of his cherishing of her. Do you see? This is a pointer to the greatest love story, the *true* love story that has the power to melt our hearts."

I showed them how the book begins with the peasant girl saying, "Let him kiss me with the kisses of his mouth!" (Song 1:2).

I asked, "Have you ever had the experience of a verse in the Bible jumping out at you, giving you just what you need? Or of God's still small voice whispering to you? Or of the Lord absolutely surprising you with circumstances that show you how mindful He is of you?"

They were all nodding, smiling.

I said, "When that happens, you've been kissed by the King."

"Oh!" they chorused.

How I loved showing these women the gospel in the Song—the great good news of how loved they are.

"At first," I continued, "when the peasant girl comes into the presence of this great shepherd-king she feels unworthy. She says, 'Do not gaze at me because I am dark' (Song 1:6)." I looked out at their faces, all the beautiful colors of our Creator's paint box. I wanted to be very clear. "This is not a reference to race. She says she's been working all day in the vineyard, darkened by the sun. She also feels unclean and unattractive. She compares herself to the dirty, weathered tents of a tribe called Kedar. You probably can identify, for you work at manual labor all day in your prison uniforms, without air conditioning and without deodorant."

"Uh-huh, sister, you got it."

All that these women had to make themselves presentable was a sliver of soap. No flattering clothes, shampoo, deodorant, makeup, and not even a decent comb, as it could be used as a weapon. (At Christmastime, if allowed, our prison ministry gives each of them deodorant and shampoo. The women are as ecstatic as if we'd given them diamond necklaces.)

"But what she says about her outward appearance is really an expression of the uncleanness she feels in her soul. The unworthiness. That is how we are when we first get close to a holy God. Like Peter, who said, 'Go away from me!' (Luke 5:8, NRSV). Or Isaiah, when he said, 'Woe is me! . . . I am a man of unclean lips' (Isaiah 6:5)."

The women nodded again. I didn't need to explain to them what it was like to feel unworthy.

I continued, "I want you to understand how the king sees this peasant girl— how the King sees you and me! He has cleansed her, made her as clean as the newly fallen snow and as pure as a lily. So he reassures her, as God does each of us, 'Behold, you are beautiful, my love; behold, you are beautiful' (Song 1:15)."

Julia, a slim blonde sitting next to me, began to tremble. I continued, saying that the bride's beauty is a refrain of the Song of Songs: "You are altogether beautiful, my love; there is no flaw in you" (Song 4:7).

Now Julia was weeping. A woman across the circle jumped up to bring her a roll of toilet paper—a staple in prison Bible studies. I didn't want to embarrass Julia by drawing attention to her, so I taught a little longer, but soon she was shaking with great heaving sobs. I paused, looked at her, and asked, "Julia, do you want to share what's going on?"

She nodded vigorously and then took a moment to compose herself. She blew her nose, wiped her eyes, and took a deep breath.

"I've always been searching for love, for the sense that I was beautiful to someone. I lost so many mother figures as a child. At eleven I turned to alcohol and then to men. I was willing to do whatever, just to get that feeling of being loved, of being thought of as beautiful. The men pretended to love me so they could use me. I did things of which I am so ashamed. Shortly after I was incarcerated, I looked in the mirror and screamed, 'I hate you! I hate you! I hate you!'"

I saw the women nodding. They identified with Julia's story, with the self-hatred and condemnation. They were listening intently as she continued.

"It is only when Christ found me that I discovered what real love is. I have been so helped by the Christian volunteers in this prison and by being assured of Christ's love and forgiveness. Just this morning, when I was walking around the track, I was overcome with gratitude and cried, 'Lord, You are so beautiful.'

"Then I thought I heard Him whisper within me, 'Julia, *you* are beautiful.' I stopped! Then I wondered if I'd imagined it. So I pleaded, 'Say it again!' But there was only silence." She started weeping again. "And then you come in here, open the Bible, tell us that God sings us a love song and keeps saying, 'Behold, you are beautiful, my love; behold, you are beautiful' (Song 1:15)."

She stopped, tears welling up, and then whispered, "He said it again!"

We all sat there in holy silence.

Finally, I whispered, "Julia, you have just been kissed by the King."

In fact, the King had kissed us all at that moment. We each were reminded once again that our God is mindful of us and loves us. We do not worship a statue or a far-off force but a God who became bone of our bones and flesh of our flesh, who dwelt among us, and who is love itself. He loves us not as we should be but as we are. This is the recurring melody of the Song: As the bridegroom loves the bride, she flourishes. As she adores him in return, she becomes increasingly beautiful, reflecting him as the moon reflects the sun.

I will never forget that night in prison when God came running to kiss His beloved. I prayed that when the women went back to their cells and pored over the Song, as I knew they would, that the Spirit would show them not just the earthly love story but Jesus Himself. And indeed, He has! When I've gone back to this facility and other prisons where I have taught the Song, the women come to me quoting verses with radiant faces, telling me how the Song has penetrated their hearts with the width, depth, and breadth of God's love.

It's not just women behind bars who need this reminder of God's deep love. As I've led this study online with women around the world, I've heard again and again the power of the Song to bring women a deeper awareness of God's love. Here are a few of the comments I've received:

> Does Jesus love me? I have been contemplating this question as my "sorrows like sea billows roll," and I have come to see that this question is key. Do I believe that He loves me even when suffering does not make sense? The Song of Songs keeps telling me He does.
> —Diane from Canada

God has used the Song of Songs to lift a veil and help me see His love in a whole new light. He calls me to come away with Him, to come away from idols, from the safety blankets I have clung to for so long.

—Staci from the Netherlands

If you desire greater intimacy with Christ, read and study the Song of Songs. It viscerally reaches places that might otherwise go untouched for a lifetime.

—Jackie from Delaware

I'm so eager for you to find refreshment and delight in the Song! This book you're reading also includes a Bible study at the end of each chapter. When we dig out truth for ourselves, we experience much greater spiritual growth. And if you have the opportunity to do this in a group, you will learn even more, for as with iron sharpening iron, the sparks will fly among you!

But I want you to get your bearings first. The Song is a deep pool of water, and I don't want anyone drowning. Let's do a short swimming lesson before we dive in.

Lesson 1: Song of Songs 1–8

 Icebreaker

Share your name and then answer these questions: In what ways might falling and staying in love with an earthly spouse be similar to falling and staying in love with Jesus? How are they different?

Watch

Watch "Enjoying Christ Constantly," the thirteen-minute online video from evangelical theologian and author Mike Reeves.[1] (See the endnotes for the direct link. If you have trouble with a link, these videos can also be found at www.deebrestin. com/hecallsyoubeautiful.) When you gather as a group, share what stood out to you. (If you already did the optional Get-Acquainted Lesson in the back, you can skip this part.)

Read Chapter 1 of *He Calls You Beautiful*

1. What stood out to you in this chapter and why? What insight into the Song of Songs did you gain?

2. What do you think Julia's heart desire was? Can you identify with that in any way? If so, explain.

3. God uses many metaphors to show us that Christianity, unlike other religions, is not rules and rituals but relationship. Find the metaphor the Bible

gives in each of the following passages and comment on what it teaches you about God. What picture does God give of Himself, and what does this teach you about Him?

a. Psalm 23

b. John 15:15

c. 1 John 3:1

d. Isaiah 62:5

4. Explain how each of the above metaphors is an escalation in intimacy. What is it about marriage that gives it the potential to be the most intimate earthly relationship of all?

5. God's plan for marriage is stated at the first marriage in Genesis 2:24 and then is repeated four times in Scripture, culminating in Ephesians 5:31–32. Read Genesis 2:20–24 and explain why you think Adam rejoiced over Eve. How does Adam's response foreshadow God's response to His bride? How does it make you feel to realize God rejoices over you?

*6. In Ephesians 5:31–32, what mystery do we learn about marriage?

7. In some ways, the Song is a mysterious puzzle! To do a puzzle well, it helps to look at the whole picture on the box before trying to put the pieces together. That's what we're going to do with the Song. Read all eight chapters of the Song as if the Song were a play. You can also listen to it read in about twenty minutes on an audio Bible.[2] This has the advantage of helping you understand who is speaking. What are your initial impressions after reading or listening to the Song?

8. *First Love.* In Song 1:1–2:14, the couple is experiencing the euphoria of new love. Describe the emotions these verses suggest.

a. Have you ever fallen in love with someone? What did it feel like?

*b. Do you remember when you first fell in love with Jesus? Or do you remember a time when His love became very real to you? If so, share what it felt like.

9. *Wilderness Love.* For most of the Song (2:15–8:4), the Shulammite woman wanders in and out of the wilderness, as we do with our relationship with God.

   a. Describe how the woman refuses the bridegroom in Song 5:2–8 and the pain that ensues.

   *b. Have you had times when you resisted the Lord and then experienced a loss of intimacy with Him? If so, share.

   c. In Song 5:8, the friends see her persisting in looking for the bridegroom despite persecution and pain. What question does that lead them to ask (see Song 5:9)?

10. *Invincible Love.* This is the stage where you know your love is here to stay. We see this in Song 8:5–14. Find phrases in that passage that show the permanency of this kind of love.

*11. What is your takeaway (what you will remember) from this lesson and discussion and why?

〜 Prayer Time

If your group is bigger than six or seven people, divide into smaller groups of three or four. Share brief prayer requests based on either what you have learned in this lesson or a need in your own life (not in Uncle Hank's neighbor's life—keep it personal). Appoint a facilitator for each group to introduce topics.

For example, the facilitator would begin, "Let's thank the Lord for something we learned about Him today." *A few give thanks. Then there is a pause.*

"Let's pray for Vicki." *A few give sentence prayers for Vicki.*

"Let's pray for Marcella." *A few give sentence prayers for Marcella.*

Facilitator closes in prayer.

Poetry to Penetrate Our Hearts

How to Read the Song of Songs

> We should read the Song in light of the bigger story that is unfolding in the whole Bible. . . . This means that the Song of Songs sings the Bible's love story.
>
> **—James M. Hamilton Jr.**

One week in July, two sisters who are friends of mine stayed with me at my home on the lake. One of my favorite things to do is swim in the refreshing waters of Green Bay. I feel cleansed and invigorated, as if God has baptized me anew!

"Would you like to swim with me?" I asked. "The water is beautiful and so clean. There's a raft a little ways out."

Eunice paused, embarrassed. "Dee, we don't know how to swim."

I was surprised. "You never learned? But why?"

"Our mother was afraid of the water. She thought if we never learned to swim, we wouldn't go near the water and drown."

I shook my head at the irrationality of such thinking. Not only would these women be much more likely to drown if they ever fell in the water, but they had missed the great joy of swimming.

Many have missed the joy of the Song because its deep waters intimidate them.

Yet following two basic hermeneutical (the science of how to interpret Scripture) principles can help.

First we need to ask, what is the genre of this Bible text? Second, how does it relate to the overarching story of the Bible? Let's start with these questions, since with this foundation beneath us, we will be prepared to experience the joy of the Song.

THE BEAUTY OF POETRY

Our creative God filled His Word with every type of literature: history, law, poetry, prophecy, parables, letters, and more. Each genre requires a slightly different approach to prevent misinterpretation of God's Word.

For example, when you read a historical book of the Bible, such as 1 Samuel or Judges, you are reading an actual account of the lives of God's people, not a prescription for how to live. Some have misinterpreted historical books, thinking God endorsed acts such as polygamy and the abuse of women when He was simply describing sins and the sorrow they created. It is in the didactic (teaching) passages and books that we see that God is opposed to polygamy, the abuse of women, and all the other sins God's people too often practiced.

The genre of the Song is poetry. Poetry is always multilayered. To miss the layers is to miss the point. Consider:

> He will cover you with his feathers,
> and under his wings you will find refuge.
> —Psalm 91:4, NIV

The Lord is using familiar images from nature to illumine a spiritual mystery. In the context of this psalm, God is compared to a mother bird. A mother bird shelters her babies at great sacrifice to herself. This earthly picture illumines a truth about God and us. But if you start focusing too much on the details—wondering, for example, what is the typical life span of a bird and what color wings the bird has—you are going to confuse the spiritual picture. We understand as we read this imagery that God is not a bird but that He protects us sacrificially as a mother bird does.

The primary earthly picture in the Song is that of a beautiful marriage in which the husband delights in the bride and she responds to that love. Even if we have not experienced this kind of love on earth, we long for it. God's love is so much greater than that of the best earthly husband. Still, marital love is something we understand, so that image is helpful in shedding light on our spiritual marriage to Christ.

Agur, compiler of a collection of proverbs found in Proverbs 30, speaks of his wonder when watching two earthly beings coming together to soar, becoming more beautiful together than either was alone.

> There are three things that are too amazing for me,
>> four that I do not understand:
> the way of an eagle in the sky,
>> the way of a snake on a rock,
> the way of a ship on the high seas,
>> and the way of a man with a maiden.
> —Proverbs 30:18–19, NIV

Agur culminates his reflections with the most wondrous mystery of all, a picture of a man and a woman. Though earthly, that relationship is still beyond his understanding. Why? Perhaps it is because the opposite sex always remains something of a mystery. Marriage, as author Mike Mason puts it, "urges us . . . out beyond our depth, out of the shallows of our own secure egocentricity and into the dangerous and unpredictable depths of a real interpersonal encounter."[1]

In the same way, God is *so* other. We cannot shape Him into what we think He should be, but we must get out of our depth into a real interpersonal encounter. This earthly picture of marriage is the closest we can come to understanding divine love. The love of a friend is great, that of a parent greater, but something about the oneness of marriage raises that love above the rest.

Some are hesitant because marriage has a sexual component. How could God use something so earthy to illustrate something so spiritual? Author Derek Kidner explains: "It is a bold and creative stroke by which God, instead of banning sexual imagery from religion, rescues and raises it to portray the ardent love and fidelity which are the essence of His covenant."[2]

Yet it is vital to realize this is a *metaphor*. Just as God is not a mother bird but uses that picture to illumine our understanding of His care, He is not a physical lover but uses that picture to penetrate our hearts with the depth of His love. To interpret this as a physical reality is not only a misunderstanding of poetry but also a diminishing of God's holiness.

The image of becoming one illumines the mystery of the Song's spiritual passion. As a husband cherishes his wife and as she responds to that love and affection, this oneness grows. This points to our becoming one with Christ, to our union and communion with Christ.

It's important to remember that the Song is not an *allegory*, where every detail represents one specific thing. Instead, the poetic words that fill the Song are *allusions* meant to stir images and experiences in our hearts and minds. Dr. Michael Reeves, president and professor at Union School of Theology in Oxford, England, explains that in an allegory, *ring* might mean only marriage. But in an allusion, *ring* could mean marriage, covenant, faithfulness, or love.[3] Likewise, "a kiss from the king" in the Song represents the many ways God is intimate with us: a word from Scripture, answered prayer, grace in a time of need, a sense of His presence. Allusions appeal to our senses, helping us *experience* Christ's love. So if you are doing this study in a small group, together you will help one another experience more by hearing what resonates in the hearts of your sisters.

When I tested this study on my weekly interactive Bible study blog,[4] my sisters had such rich insights as God's Spirit rang bells in their hearts. I remember a woman named Susan writing about how to read the Song, and I knew even then that I had to share her words with you!

> Take your Bible and open it to the Song of Songs. Settle down in your
> favorite chair, preferably near a window so you can pause to look outside
> at the beauty of God's creation. Bring along all of your senses, because
> you are going to meet and experience Him in a way you never have before.
> Take in the fragrance, for His very name is like perfume poured out. Are
> you bruised by life? Feel your skin and read that His name is also like a
> soothing balm. Sit in His shade and allow Him to feed you with sweet
> fruit. Hear Him knocking at the door of your heart, saying, "Open to me,
> my sister, my love, my dove, my perfect one." Think of His great love and

sacrifice for you even when you loved Him not, and feel with your hands the myrrh that He has left on the doorknob. See Him in all His splendor as He comes up from the desert like a column of smoke, powerful and strong with arms like rods of gold, yet gentle and tender as you slip your hand in His. Then imagine walking with Him, hand in hand, through the vineyards and gardens as He shows you your future with Him in a time when the winter will be over and everything will be in bloom.

—Susan from Ohio

Susan allowed the poetic earthly pictures to take her to a different realm. This is the power of poetry.

The Big Story

One thing that ties the Bible's different genres together is the big story of the Bible, from Genesis to Revelation. In the opening to her *Jesus Storybook Bible,* Sally Lloyd-Jones explains that the Bible is not really a book of rules or morals or heroes but rather a love story: "The Bible is most of all a Story. It's an adventure story about a young Hero who comes from a far country to win back his lost treasure. It's a love story about a brave Prince who leaves his palace, his throne—everything—to rescue the one he loves. It's like the most wonderful of fairy tales that has come true in real life!"[5]

This is the gospel—and this is the whole story of the Bible from Genesis to Revelation. So of course this love story of the Song would need to fit into the big story. It is like an impressionistic painting, evoking emotion about the most excellent of subjects: the union of Christ and His bride, of which Puritan theologian Jonathan Edwards says, "Marriage and conjugal love was but a shadow."[6]

This marriage metaphor is for singles and marrieds, men and women. All believers are the bride of Christ, just as all believers are sons of God. One man shared how grasping this enhanced his understanding of the Song:

I'd thought of the Song as being primarily about marriage. However, there's so much I was missing. After all, the Bible from beginning to end is a cohesive story of God's love for His people. From that viewpoint, I can see Him pursuing me, rescuing me from my own sense of inadequacy, delighting in me, and declaring His love for me. It is amazing to think of myself as His beloved.

—Jon from South Carolina

With poetry genre and the overarching story of the Bible in mind, let's consider the Song's two main characters.

CAST OF CHARACTERS

Who is this bridegroom? The bridegroom is a shepherd (see Song 1:7–8), yet he is also a king of great wealth and splendor (see Song 3:11). He is an earthly bridegroom, yet he is so much more. Mike Reeves turns to the wedding scene in Song 3:6, where the bride is being led by the groom through the wilderness with columns of smoke.

"This is no ordinary romance," Reeves says. "This is about the romance between Christ and His bride, His people, the Church. And so the song is all about union with Christ."[7] This is no ordinary bridegroom. This is One whose love is stronger than death, who is the fairest of ten thousand to our souls.

And this is no ordinary bride: she is often compared to a vineyard, which, as Reeves points out, is the same metaphor God uses when speaking of His people.[8] In Isaiah 5, the Lord sings a love song about His beloved vineyard. He tells how He cleared it of stones, planted it with choice vines, built a water tower in the midst of it, yet it produced only wild grapes, grapes of bloodshed and injustice. But the vineyard in the Song eventually is filled with sweet fruit, as the bride abides in the shelter of the bridegroom's love.

This metaphor of a vineyard also reminds us of Jesus's words that He is the vine and we are the branches and that fruitfulness comes from abiding in Him and allowing Him to abide in us (see John 15). Do you see? Both the marriage metaphor and the vineyard metaphor illustrate the way to have vibrancy in our Christian lives; they *both* point to union and communion with Christ.

The bride is an individual—a cherished one among many—yet she is also corporate, made up of every tribe and nation. The reason the pronouns vacillate between singular and plural in the Song is because *this* bride is the bride of Christ, who is both individual and corporate. She is like a single rose of Sharon, yet she is also as formidable and beautiful as an army with banners.

This is no ordinary bride. This is the beautiful bride of Christ.

There are others in the cast, such as the daughters of Jerusalem and the bride's brothers, but we will consider them as the story unfolds.

Next, I want you to grasp the basic story line. Because the Song is a poetic song, it doesn't move strictly chronologically the way prose might. It leaps back and forth, repeating a refrain of desire, the way we repeat a chorus of a song. Though the Song keeps repeating this chorus, there is still a basic movement in the Song through three stages of love.

THREE STAGES OF LOVE

The first chapter and a half of the Song is the euphoria of *first love.* By the middle of chapter 2, the bride has moved into the *wilderness love,* where she finds pain, confusion, and also growth. For most of the rest of the Song, she moves in and out of the wilderness. But by the close of the book, we read,

> Who is that coming up from the wilderness,
>> leaning on her beloved?
>> —Song 8:5

She is experiencing an intimacy with her beloved that is even better than euphoria of first love. It is the promised land of *invincible love.*

This is where God wants to take you, to the promised land of invincible love: a land of intimacy, contentment, and inextinguishable joy. The Song is a gift to help you trust His love and move into a land that is as close to Eden and the coming new heaven and earth as anyone can experience in this fallen world.

The Song is not the only place in Scripture that uses the typical stages of an earthly marriage—first love, a wilderness time of struggling, and finally joy and contentment—to help us understand our relationship with God. For example, God says,

I remember the devotion of your youth,
    your love as a bride,
how you followed me in the wilderness,
    in a land not sown.
    —Jeremiah 2:2

But then witness His heartbreak at their defection as He asks,

What wrong did your fathers find in me
    that they went far from me?
    —Jeremiah 2:5

We are euphoric in our season of first love with God. But then the rose-colored glasses come off and we see that life is still full of trouble. We become angry with our Bridegroom for not snapping His fingers and ending our trouble. We grumble and complain.

Many marriages end in the wilderness, just as many of God's people rebelled against Him in the wilderness. God allowed those rebellious believers to die there. Why? "God was not pleased with most of them; their bodies were scattered over the desert. Now these things occurred as examples to keep us from setting our hearts on evil things as they did" (1 Corinthians 10:5–6, NIV).

It was never God's heart for any of His own to die in the wilderness. Instead, the wilderness is intended to transform us into what He intended: individuals who are grounded in Him, strong and glorious. That can happen—most of the time in our marriages and always in our relationship with the Lord—if we trust and persevere. Then, like the bride in the Song, we discover the sweet promised land of invincible love on the other side.

WHY SOLOMON?

Before we go further, I want to address two controversies about the Song.

The first has to do with Solomon, a most controversial man.

I once facilitated a Bible study for pastors' wives and women pastors in our community. When we began our study of Ecclesiastes, a book also attributed to Solomon, one of the women said, "Well, you have to take anything written by Solomon with a grain of salt, because he had seven hundred wives and three hundred concubines."

Another woman said, "But all Scripture is inspired by God, so I don't think we should take *any* of it 'with a grain of salt.'"

Here we are again, shocked that God would choose such an unfaithful husband to represent the Bridegroom, in whom there is no shadow of turning. Yet, clearly, the opening verse of the Song states, "The Song of Songs, which is Solomon's."

Some have tried to solve the puzzle by concluding that Solomon's sin of acquiring a thousand women disqualifies him from being either the author or the bridegroom in the Song. It's true that we cannot positively know he was the author, although it certainly sounds like Solomon and he was known for his 1,005 songs (see 1 Kings 4:32). But we can know positively that he represents the earthly bridegroom, for he is named in the wedding scene:

> Go out, O daughters of Zion,
>   and look upon King Solomon,
> with the crown with which his mother
>   crowned him
>   on the day of his wedding,
>   on the day of the gladness of his heart.
> —Song 3:11

So how are we to solve this puzzle?

One theory is that this is a picture of Solomon as he wished he had been. Ecclesiastes shows us a sadder but wiser man who looks back at the folly of his youth, including those many women. Ecclesiastes has been called the saddest song, as it pictures one who tried to find meaning "under the sun" apart from God, building castles and collecting harems. Vanity of vanities! Here, in the sweetest song of the Song of Songs, Solomon has a chance to tell us a story of how his life could have been had he obeyed God.

But often when we fail and fail to get a piece to fit in a puzzle, it is because the piece that we kept trying to force into the blue sky slides, without a hitch, into the blue sea!

Theologian Ellen F. Davis, in the Westminster Bible Companion series, asks us to consider Solomon's superlative achievement in life for she "suspects that the most important reason the Song is called 'Solomon's' lies precisely in this association with the Temple. . . . The cumulative effect of the language and images of the Song is to orient us toward that place of ultimate intimacy with God." Davis says, "Look behind the Temple building itself to the spiritual reality for which it stands. The Song points to the possibility of intimate encounter with God in this world." Do you see? Like the Temple, the Song also points us to the possibility of an intimate encounter with God! Now the phrase "the Song of Song's which is Solomon's" makes perfect sense.[9]

Also, God chose Solomon to build His temple because Solomon was a man of peace. The temple represented a way God's sinful people could find peace and a relationship with a holy God. The psalmist writes,

> How lovely is your dwelling place,
>   O LORD of hosts!
> My soul longs, yes, faints
>   for the courts of the LORD;
> my heart and flesh sing for joy
>   to the living God.
>   —Psalm 84:1–2

It is not so much the physical beauty of the temple that the psalmist longs for but the fact that it is the "dwelling place" of God. The psalmist's heart will not be satisfied until he can experience intimacy with "the living God." The purpose of Solomon's temple was to provide a door for intimacy with God.

Could it be that the purpose of Solomon's Song is the same? To open a door, through word pictures, for intimacy with a loving God. It has been said that the longest eighteen inches is from our heads to our hearts. The Song, empowered with word pictures, can help our knowledge of God drop to our hearts.

Is the Song Primarily About Marriage or About Christ and His Bride?

There is a second controversy that I believe looms above the first: Which is more important, the love song between the man and the woman or the love song between Christ and His bride?

Because Ephesians tells us that marriage is meant to point to the mystery of Christ and His bride, most scholars agree that the Song offers both an earthly and a spiritual picture. The controversy is over which picture is preeminent. Your perspective on that profoundly impacts your interpretation of the Song.

Up until about the 1800s, the position of the church was that the Song of Songs was about Christ and His relationship with the church.[10] Nothing, pastors thought, was more important for their flock in overcoming trial and temptation than seeing how much Christ cherished them.

Many of the ancient scholars also did not refer to earthly marriage at all when discussing the Song. It could be that they didn't because they felt it was self-evident. Or, it is possible, as pastor and theologian R. C. Sproul thinks, that the sensual imagery of the Song embarrassed them and they tried to get around it by spiritualizing everything.[11] For example, in the fifth century, Cyril of Alexandria said that "when the woman describes her love lying between her two breasts like a sachet of myrrh, what she was really talking about was Jesus standing between the Old and New Testaments."[12] This approach was blind to the picture of earthly marriage.

But today I believe we have a much more serious myopia. If you hear the Song taught on at all, it is almost exclusively focused on marriage and the marriage bed. Indeed, the Song holds insights for marriage, which we will see as we progress. When marriage is the *only* focus, Christ is lost—except perhaps as an addendum where singles are told to remember that Jesus is their Bridegroom, a consolation prize of sorts. This one-sided approach has lent itself to wild interpretations as well. Some preachers sexualize everything, treating the Song as soft porn, turning it into a graphic sex manual. With this approach, it becomes impossible to see Christ at all.

I believe the primary focus of the Song, as with every other book in the Bible, is the relationship between God and His people. But whether *you see* the primary focus as a husband and wife or as Jesus and His bride, I know you will be blessed by seeing both. And if you hold both views together, you will be less likely to misinterpret, as some ancient and modern theologians have done, polarizing into one interpretation or the other.

The ancients forbade the reading of the Song of Songs before the age of thirty. But was that because it was just about sex? Or might they have feared that the young would see *only* sex, tittering like schoolboys, trampling upon the pearl of great price? That seems to be where our sexualized world is today. Images of sexual promiscuity have so flooded our land that many believers can no longer imagine how God could use *this* metaphor to communicate a deep truth to us. The trumpet of perversion drowns out the still small voice of God.

If you have been taught that the Song is *only* about marriage and sex, you may feel hesitant at first to consider another interpretation. But I'd encourage you to give the Lord a chance to reveal Himself to you in the Song. The language of the Song is very private, and yet that is also key to its power. Indeed, we can actually hear the voice of Jesus rejoicing over us, just as Isaiah 62:5 says He does.

The most reliable commentary on Scripture is Scripture itself. It was the preponderance of parallel texts that convinced Jonathan Edwards that the Song was a divine song respecting the union between the Messiah and the church.[13] I believe you will be greatly refreshed to see that you are more cherished than you dared to dream. The Song will help press the truth into your heart, for it is one thing to be *told* that God rejoices over us as a bridegroom rejoices over His bride, but it is quite another thing to *see* it.

Yet we must approach the Song of Songs with reverence. According to Dr. Ellen Davis, "The Talmud preserves a rabbinic saying that anyone who treats the Song of Songs lightly (as a mere drinking song) 'forfeits his place in the world to come and will bring evil into the world and *imperil the welfare of all humankind.*'"[14] Although I wouldn't go that far, I am deeply grieved that in our hypersexualized culture, the Song has frequently been interpreted only as a sex manual. How vital that we see the metaphor and not focus exclusively on the earthly picture.

Puritan Richard Sibbes writes, "As none entered into the holy of holies but the high priest, . . . so none can enter into the mystery of this Song of songs, but such as have more near communion with Christ."[15] C. S. Lewis, in his final interview, commented on how much strength the saints and martyrs of the past had found in the Song, but then he gave a caution: *"What is meat for a grown person might be unsuited to the palate of a child."*[16]

You don't need to have walked with the Lord for many years to study the Song, but you need enough hunger for God to be motivated to find the time to truly study it. Otherwise you might jump to conclusions, misunderstand the purpose of the Song, and bring confusion and discord to your small group.

What I appreciate about the growing number of contemporary theologians who see Christ as the primary emphasis in the Song is that they neither deny the earthly picture of the marriage bed nor sexualize the Song to the point that the spiritual picture of Christ and His Bride is lost.

Once I had an opportunity to ask songwriter Michael Card if he, as a man, could relate to this metaphor of the bride, since both men and women are the bride of Christ. He said that he could, for he understood how much he cherished his own bride, Susan. And then he said, and I think this is significant,

> I don't think Scripture is going to give us a metaphor that the Holy Spirit cannot help us relate to. I don't ever want to say that there is a part of the Bible that is not for me or not for you. I hope I never become so sexualized that I can't see the meaning here.[17]

Our world is obsessed with sex, particularly sex outside of the marriage. Pray you will not be squeezed into the world's mold but that you will have eyes to see the beauty of the marriage bed as God designed it and then the sacred picture to which it points.

A side benefit to studying the Song of Songs is that it has the power to enhance your marriage, helping you to see its beauty, including the beauty of an undefiled marriage bed. Our world has lost its moorings on what love really is, jettisoning the foundational values of purity, faithfulness, the mystery of otherness, and the dignity of marriage. Speaking of the world's distortion of sexuality, theology professor James Hamilton asks, "What if there was something so beautiful it could break the spell of all that eye-candy? What if there was something so satisfying it would empower us to hear the siren song for what it is—an invitation to ruin and misery with the smoke of your destruction going up forever and ever?"[18]

Indeed, the Song has the power to break the world's spell and give you something so much better, *because* marriage points to an eternal relationship with Jesus. That understanding also rescues, and indeed raises, the marriage bed. The psalmist says, "The unfolding of your words gives light" (Psalm 119:130), and I know that as the Song is unfolded, you will be drawn closer to not only your eternal Bridegroom but also your earthly bridegroom and find delight, as God intended, in the marriage bed.

We do not wrestle with flesh and blood but with the rulers of darkness, and it does not surprise me that the demons would target God's plan for marriage and sexuality with such ferocity. Even they seem to sense that this picture points to the deep love of God for His bride—a beautiful reality the demons do not want us to comprehend.

THE DEPTH OF GOD'S LOVE

The parables tell of a bridegroom returning unexpectedly at midnight and of a king who held a wedding feast for his son. The prophets tell stories of a brokenhearted bridegroom who loves a faithless bride. And the poets sing of a great shepherd-king who fell passionately in love with a peasant maiden. The last love story is so intimate that it can make readers blush. Yet, in a day of superficial relationships, it taps into the deepest longing of our hearts. We long to know and be known, to love and be loved, to cherish and be cherished.

God's love for us is passionate, and He longs for a passionate bride in return. The word *passion* has also come to mean the suffering of Christ, as His love was so *intense* for us that He went to the cross.

If people could be awakened to see that the Bible is not a book of rules or heroes but a *love* story, the story of the One who left everything to rescue His bride, might it finally penetrate their hearts?

And if you, who may indeed know the Lord, could see, hear, feel, and taste this love, how might your relationship with Him be transformed?

When we doubt God's love, we quench the Spirit, slow down the process of transformation, and wander for years in the wilderness, worshiping idols. Instead of running to the Lover of our souls, we run to lesser things—to good gifts like food or friends, sports or sex—which can delight us but utterly fail in themselves to deliver us from our loneliness and deception.

Is it unusual for a believer to doubt God's love? Not at all. Tim Keller, former pastor of Redeemer Presbyterian Church in New York City and cofounder of the Gospel Coalition, says that such doubt is his biggest problem. This is a man God has used so mightily, and yet he too has times when God's love for him appears dim.

I am convinced that believing in God's love is the struggle of every believer. Though it may seem shocking that God would share such an intimate love story in His Word, it is what He knows our doubting hearts desperately need.

I have found that true intimacy with God comes more frequently for me through the Song than through most books of the Bible, for the Song is a love letter. I encourage you, as you read this book, to read the Song aloud chapter by chapter. Linger over it as you would a love letter.

The Song is filled with sounds and word pictures meant to help you sense God's love. Poetry is prose condensed, meant to penetrate the heart with arrows of love. So speak this poem aloud, linger over its meaning, and allow this living Word to arouse your passion for the Lord.

The Song reminds me of a dance, for it is God who initiates, and then as we allow Him to take us in His arms, He takes our breath away by swirling us about the dance floor. He sings to us a song, a gospel love song. A Song of all songs.

Shall we dance?

LESSON 2: SONG OF SONGS 1–8

 Icebreaker

Divide into pairs and then interview the other person for two or three minutes each. Then each of you will introduce the other to the whole group. Ask some questions that probe deeper, such as, what do you love about your life? What are you passionate about?

 Watch

To prepare your heart for this study, watch the online music video of Martin Smith's "Song of Solomon."[19] When you gather as a group, share your thoughts on it.

Read Chapter 2 of *He Calls You Beautiful*

1. What insight did you gain by looking into the Song?

2. What stood out to you in this chapter and why?

3. The Song is poetry, and poetry is always multilayered. With this in mind, look at Song 2:14. What is the primary earthly picture? How does this illumine how Jesus feels about you and what He wants from you?

4. Read Agur's poetry in Proverbs 30:18–19. Explain how the first three pictures show the beauty of two becoming one. Why is the last beyond his understanding?

5. The Song is filled with allusions meant to ring many bells of recognition in our spirits. This is different from allegory, in which one thing directly represents another thing. Describe what the following images make you think of. The first one has been started for you:

   a. *Your love is better than wine.* Wine might ring bells of the Holy Spirit, joy, plenty, celebration, life, and more.

   *b. *My beloved is like a gazelle.*

   *c. *O my dove, in the clefts of the rock.*

6. After His resurrection, Jesus walked beside two disciples on the road to Emmaus and revealed to them that *He* is the big story of the Bible. Read Luke 24:13–24. Why were the disciples so sad? What humor do you see in this historical account?

a. In Luke 24:25–27, what does Jesus explain to the disciples?

*b. Can you think of ways that Moses (see Exodus 12), David (see Psalm 22), or Isaiah (see Isaiah 53) foreshadowed Christ? Choose one of these examples (or another one) and explain how this person points to Christ or His gospel.

7. In Song 3:6, the bridegroom leads his bride though the wilderness with "columns of smoke." What picture does this bring to mind, and what does this show you?

8. What unusual perfume is the bridegroom wearing in Song 3:6? What might be the significance of this in light of God's big story throughout Scripture?

9. Psalm 45, as we will later see, is the Song in miniature. When Psalm 45 is quoted in Hebrews 2:9, the Bridegroom is named. Who is it?

10. To what does the Shulammite liken herself in Song 1:6? Compare this verse to Isaiah 5:1–2. What do you see?

11. In most of the Song, the Shulammite seems like an individual, yet in Song 6:10 she's compared to a whole army. What does this tell you about her identity?

12. Why is Solomon a controversial choice to represent a faithful bridegroom?

13. Perhaps Solomon was chosen for his greatest achievement rather than his greatest failure. Read 1 Chronicles 22:6–10. What was Solomon's achievement, what did it represent, and why might this be linked to the purpose of the Song?

*14. The other controversy is which picture in the Song should be preeminent: marriage or the relationship between Christ and His bride. Whether or not you know what you think about this yet, how might the two pictures enhance one another?

15. What is your takeaway from this lesson and why?

 Prayer Time

Divide into clusters, share your requests, and then have a facilitator in each group lead you in a time of thanksgiving and supplication.

First Love

And Can It Be?

Kiss Me

A Refrain of Desire

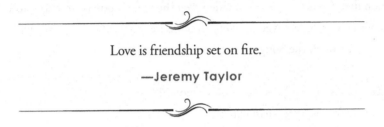

Love is friendship set on fire.

—Jeremy Taylor

remember waiting eagerly for a first kiss from my future husband, Steve. It would signal that our relationship was moving past friendship. I knew after our first date that he was the man I wanted to spend the rest of my life with, but how did he feel? I could tell he enjoyed our in-depth conversations and our laughter together, but did he *desire* me?

Within a month after our first date, we went to a Valentine's Day party my sorority held. Each couple was supposed to come as famous lovers; we were assigned Helen of Troy and Paris. That was a little awkward since we were just friends, but Steve went along with it good-naturedly. He taped pictures of the city of Paris to his V-neck sweater, since he wouldn't be caught in a leotard! I went to a salon to have my hair put in an updo with flowers, and I wore a flowing white gown.

I was aware of Steve's penetrating gaze all evening. When we left the party and walked onto Northwestern University's lovely campus, the snow was sparkling under the moon and stars. He turned to me and took my face in his hands, and I thought, *Oh my—he's going to kiss me.* And oh, he did. I replayed the moment over and over in my mind during the next few days. *We are more than friends.* And then, all I wanted was *more.* I would watch the clock, waiting for our date, fantasizing, as did the Shulammite woman, about the "kisses of his mouth." His kisses electrified me. All I could think about day and night was Steve.

Kathy and Tim Keller were friends for a long time. *Too long*, Kathy thought. Frustrated, she finally decided to give Tim "the speech" about taking her for granted and leading her on without making a deeper commitment, but he stopped her midsentence by leaning down and kissing her. The argument was over.[1]

Is anything more electrifying than a first kiss? And a kiss of desire is where we begin the Song of Songs. We might expect our story to begin chronologically when Solomon first meets the peasant maiden. But the Song is poetry and not prose, so it opens with a refrain, a passionate refrain of desire that will repeat, with variations, all the way through the Song:

> Let him kiss me with the kisses of his mouth!
> For your love is better than wine;
> > your anointing oils are fragrant;
> your name is oil poured out;
> > therefore virgins love you.
> Draw me after you; let us run.
> > The king has brought me into his chambers.
> —Song 1:2–4

This poetic refrain of desire illumines the spiritual picture, for passionate desire is what we need most if we are to have vibrancy in our relationship with Jesus. As John Eldredge says, "Christianity is not an invitation to become a moral person. . . . Christianity begins with an invitation to *desire*."[2]

THE KISSES OF HIS MOUTH

We might be tempted to see reading Scripture as a duty to check off. The Song leads us back to having the attitude Christian evangelist George Mueller refers to when he writes, "I consider it my greatest need before God and man to get my soul happy before the Lord each day before I see anybody."[3] We need to be kissed! We need to be awakened to just how good God is. We need to come to our time with God with an attitude of expectancy, raising our face to His.

God longs for us to be alert to His kisses all through the day: the sense of wonder when we wake to a brand-new day with no mistakes, the joy we feel when we walk in His love, the grace that washes over us when we truly repent. All these are evidences of God being in relationship with His responsive bride.

Author Jamie Lash, who has a ministry with Messianic Jews, writes about what a kiss can represent: "According to rabbinic tradition, [a spiritual kiss] is a living word of prophecy. . . . Have you ever had the experience of reading or hearing something from the Bible which suddenly came alive to you, literally jumping off the page, and you knew that God was speaking to *you*? If you have, you've been kissed by God."[4]

The Shulammite woman asks for the "kisses of his mouth." What is the significance of such kisses? Certainly they are more passionate than air kisses or a kiss on the cheek, but there is more. Do you remember when Miriam and Aaron claimed to have heard from God and opposed their brother Moses's marriage to an Ethiopian woman? (Their opposition might have been based on racial prejudice.) God came to Moses's defense, praising Moses and saying, "With him I speak mouth to mouth, clearly, and not in riddles" (Numbers 12:8). I believe God was confirming that Moses had heard from Him clearly, unlike his siblings.

At times I see something in the Word that I had not understood before and my spirit comes alive, not just because I now see with clarity, but also because I sense the very presence of God revealing it to me. He is being intimate with me.

God doesn't kiss me every time I read His Word, but I try to remember to ask Him to do so. Even when I forget, sometimes He delightfully surprises me. It reminds me of how Steve would sometimes come up behind me when I was working in the kitchen, turn me around, and kiss me soundly.

One of the greatest weaknesses we have individually and corporately is lack of desire for the Lord. We have church programs but not shared passion. We have routines but not longing. We sometimes treat God like a spiritual vending machine instead of a Person who desires intimacy with us.

The Song shows us the kind of bride God desires, one who is yearning to be kissed "with the kisses of his mouth" (1:2), to sit under "his shadow" (2:3), and to hold him and "not let him go" (3:4). She desires him because his presence is better than any earthly gift.

This is the desire Adam had when he walked and talked with God in Eden.

But then the serpent slithered in, planting doubt. Eve fell first, and Adam followed. Work became toilsome, childbirth painful, marriage filled with strife. Bodies decayed and died, and the Garden of Eden was lost. Worst of all, Adam and Eve no longer walked and talked with God in perfect intimacy.

We each have followed in Eve's footsteps, listening to the Enemy, choosing our own way, valuing autonomy over closeness with God. The Fall broke many things, including the marriage bed, which God meant to be pure and undefiled (see Hebrews 13:4)—a place, when protected, where the marriage covenant could be regularly renewed.

The Song of Songs gives us a picture of the world redeemed. All the sad effects of the Fall are repaired and reversed.[5] No longer is sex polluted; it again becomes beautiful in the marriage bed. As before the Fall, now husband and wife are naked and unashamed with one another. Instead of trying to control the other for selfish gain, they are now selflessly devoted to each other. The land, instead of being choked with thorns, is now a garden: the winter is past, the time of singing has come, and flowers appear on the earth (see Song 2:11–12). And man and woman, instead of being banished from the garden, *live* in a garden, walking with a God who delights in them, who longs to see their faces and hear the sound of their voices.

This is the picture in the Song and is indeed the sure promise that runs through all of Scripture. The best is yet to come. According to Dr. Ellen Davis, "The Song is about repairing the damage done by the first disobedience in Eden."[6] James Hamilton shares that "the Song sings of what we would long for in our hearts if we knew how to hope for heaven."[7]

But we don't have to wait for heaven to taste it on earth. A kiss from the King can wake us to see glimpses of God's restoration here and now—and create in us a desire for more.

The Gospel Kiss

Snow White ate a poisoned apple that the wicked queen gave her. Just like Eve, Snow White was deceived, took and ate, and experienced "death." She fell into a coma and was placed in a glass coffin. Only a kiss from the prince could rescue her.

In the same way, the Bible says we were "dead" before Christ awakened us. He awakened us with a "gospel kiss," wooing us to Him. He brought light to our darkness, life to our souls, and desire to our hearts.

That gospel kiss in my own life electrified me the same way Steve's first kiss did. I knelt to surrender to the God who'd been wooing me. All I was expecting in that moment was to be delivered from the fear of hell. But oh! He came running, enfolding me in His love. I was on fire. All I wanted to do was serve this amazing God who was real and personal and brought healing to my soul.

I remember running to the pastor of the church Steve and I had begun attending as a married couple and saying, "I've *got* to do something. How can I show God I love Him?" Pastor Reed, desperate for help, quickly made me his part-time volunteer secretary, something this very right-brained woman is *not* gifted at doing, but I was *driven* by my desire to serve God. So while my toddler pushed his riding giraffe round and round the office, I did my best at filing and accounting, often mis-filing and mis-accounting! (I think my pastor breathed a sigh of relief when a second pregnancy led to my resignation. Passion is good, but it must be channeled according to our gifts!)

How I love to hear the stories of God waking His princesses and princes from their death sleep with a kiss, leading them to a passion and eagerness they've never had before. Recently I heard a stirring testimony from a young woman in Iran who grew up in a Muslim family. No person told Nastaran Farahani about Jesus, but God Himself awakened her with a gospel kiss. She was just sixteen when, while taking a shower, she heard a voice: "Repent. I am going to wash you of your sin."

Nastaran didn't understand, yet she held those words in her heart. Then her sister from Holland visited. A friend had had a vision that her sister was to go to her family, and another friend had given her the necessary plane ticket. When Nastaran's sister arrived, she opened her bag, took out her Bible, and said, "I believe in Jesus." Her family began to cry in dismay.

But Nastaran said, "I believe in Jesus. I do not know how. But I believe." Shortly after that, through a dream to her father and a vision to her mother, her parents too received the gospel kiss and put their trust in Christ.[8]

The gospel kiss is needed to awaken us in the beginning of our faith, but we also need continual kisses to prevent us from losing our grasp on the gospel. Martin

Luther is credited with having said that the default mode of the human heart is to retreat to works of righteousness—trying to earn God's love, His kisses. As we try to save ourselves, we keep forgetting that Jesus paid it all in full.

I see this struggle all the time at the prisons. I remember talking to Tammy, who had served ten years of her thirty-year sentence for shaking her baby. Though Tammy had become a Christian, she told me, with tears, "I know Jesus forgives me, but I can't forgive myself."

"Tammy, it isn't even possible to grant forgiveness to yourself. It has to come from outside yourself," I told her.

She was quiet.

"Tammy, I understand your struggle. When my husband died of cancer, I began to lose my grip on the gospel. I had thoughts like, *I deserve this. I'm such an idiot. I fail God every day.* But one day I was listening to a preacher who said something I already knew but somehow had forgotten. He said, 'When a Christian suffers, it is never because God is punishing him. Jesus took it at the cross and he said, "It is finished" (John 19:30).'" I took Tammy's hands in mine and said, "Tammy, it is finished. Jesus paid for your sin in full. He forgives you completely. He says, 'You are altogether beautiful, my love; there is no flaw in you' (Song 4:7)."

I saw the hope in her eyes. God's repeated gospel kiss was bringing her back to life.

BETTER THAN WINE

Recently my eldest son, JR, celebrated a milestone birthday. His wife, Dianne, arranged for one of his closest friends, Eric, to join them on a spiritual retreat at a cabin in Brown County, Indiana—a breathtaking spot in autumn. Eric's plane from Virginia was delayed, so by the time they started the drive to the cabin, it was a minute past midnight, and the first minute of JR's milestone birthday, when JR drove into a speed trap. Though he was going 55 and his GPS said 55, the lights behind him were flashing and JR pulled over. The policeman said the rate had slowed to 50. JR's wife, hoping for mercy, told the policeman it was her husband's birthday. The policeman took the information from JR's license and went back to his squad car.

JR was feeling saddened that this was how this anticipated celebration was starting. Eric said, "Brother, don't let this steal your joy!"

JR looked in his mirror at the still flashing police lights and said, "Well, I guess his lights do sort of look like birthday candles."

In response, Eric began to sing, "Happy birthday to you," and Dianne joined in. Then they began to laugh. Their singing and laughter floated through the open window.

The policeman came up to the car and asked, "Have you been drinking?"

Eric, wanting to be authentic, said, "Sir, I did have a glass of wine on the plane coming in two hours ago."

JR said, "Sir, I don't drink."

Eric said, "Sir, we love Jesus and we're just full of the joy of the Lord."

The policeman lifted an eyebrow, paused, and then gave JR a warning.

Both wine and the Holy Spirit can intoxicate, making an individual joyful and bold. But there is a key difference. Wine does it by suppressing the truth and our natural inhibitions. The Holy Spirit does it by illumining the truth of Christ and giving us confidence that He is with us. There is indeed a buzz when you experience the joy of the Lord, a joy the world cannot understand. It is a joy that is better than the things of this world:

> You have put more joy in my heart
> > than they have when their grain and wine abound.
> —Psalm 4:7

On an earthly level, when the peasant woman says, "Your love is better than wine," she is speaking of the intoxication of new love. Several Hebrew words are translated "love" in the Song. Here the Hebrew word is *dôd*, derived from the word for "boiling pot." When the word is used in the plural, as it is here, it means sexual intimacy. (Hebrew words often sound like what they represent. Say *dôd, dôd, dôd, dôd* quickly, and you'll hear a boiling pot.)

I quoted John Donne's famous poem "Batter My Heart, Three-Person'd God" in the opening pages of this book because he captures this metaphor of passion perfectly and powerfully. Here is the first part of the close of Donne's famous poem:

Dearly I love you, and would be lov'd fain,
But am betrothed unto your enemy: Divorce me,
    untie or break that knot again.

Donne is saying that he dearly loves the Lord but feels married, or tied, to God's enemy. He pleads for God to "divorce" him, to break his tie with the devil.

I understand. I can get so discouraged when I repeat a sin of which I have repented! Why do I lose my temper with my little grandchildren, whom I love so much? Why do I graze on food that I know I don't need? Why does my heart not break for the things that break the heart of God?

I cannot deliver myself. Who will deliver me? Only Jesus. So I cry for those ungodly ties to be broken. But that is not enough—unless God comes to me, I will never be free, for heart idols cannot be removed but only replaced! I will never be chaste unless God ravishes me with His love.

Donne's words continue:

Take me to you, imprison me, for I,
Except you enthrall me, never shall be free,
Nor ever chaste, except you ravish me.

These are strong words—to be enthralled, to be ravished—but that is what we need to be set free from the siren songs of our idols. And this is why the repeated refrain of the Song is *desire*. Desire for God is the secret of setting us free from the Enemy, who seeks to destroy us. Do you want to be set free? Then learn what it means to be ravished by God.

ALL SENSES AWAKE

Although the peasant woman is drawn to her bridegroom physically, she is also drawn to his character. "Your name is oil poured out," she says (Song 1:3). In Scripture, anointing someone with oil was a sign of blessing from the Holy Spirit and literally wrapped a person in fragrance. *Fragrance* is such a good word picture for God's enveloping presence, like the presence we feel when His peace comes in the midst of sorrow.

Years ago, my dear friend Twila's newborn baby died. As she sat before the Lord in tremendous grief, she felt a gentle hand placed upon the crown of her head and then the feeling of warm oil flowing down from the top of her head all the way over her body and down to her feet, soothing, soothing, soothing. To the Shulammite, Solomon's name, which meant "peace," represented his character to her and soothed her. Likewise, the very name of Jesus is like soothing oil, for it represents so much: Savior, Prince of Peace, Counselor, Lamb of God, the Alpha and Omega.

I often feel God's presence in close Christian fellowship, when I am sharing with kindred spirits the things of the Lord. It is as David writes,

> Behold, how good and pleasant it is
>> when brothers dwell in unity!
> It is like the precious oil on the head,
>> running down on the beard,
> on the beard of Aaron,
>> running down on the collar of his robes!
> —Psalm 133:1–2

When the Shulammite woman likens her lover's love to wine and his name to fragrant oil being poured out, she is bringing in all the senses: hearing, seeing, touching, smelling, and tasting. Our faith, too, is not just head knowledge. *All* our senses are involved in the intimacy of knowing God—an intimacy expressed through the intense physicality of the Song.

In Marilynne Robinson's novel *Home,* the protagonist, Jack, is struggling to have this deep core awareness of God. He says to his sister, Glory, "It is possible to know the great truths without feeling the truth of them. That's where the problem lies. In my case."[9]

Jack understands that faith hasn't fallen to his heart. He is aware of his need, though so many of us are not.

Even many ministers and chaplains may not be aware of the need for faith to be in not just the head but also the heart. My brother-in-law, John Frahm, was a Lutheran pastor for many years. When his church went through Alpha—the outreach video program that has been so anointed by God to awaken sleeping souls worldwide—he said that by the sixth video everything in his head fell to his heart.

He wept in repentance at having led without really knowing the Lord, and he wept because for the first time, he was *experiencing* the love of God.

Even the Hebrew word for "know" is used in Scripture to express both sexual intimacy and true saving faith, faith that has dropped to the heart. For example, these verses use the same Hebrew word, *yada,* for "know":

> Adam *knew* his wife, and she conceived and bore Cain.
> —Genesis 4:1

> Behold, you shall call a nation that you do not *know,*
> and a nation that did not *know* you shall run to you.
> —Isaiah 55:5

How good God is to give us a book like the Song of Songs, which helps us connect our head knowledge of God with our heart longing for Him.

THE CHAMBERS OF THE KING

"The king has brought me into his chambers," the maiden says (Song 1:4). In this euphoria of new love before the wedding, it sometimes seems as if the maiden is describing sexual intimacy. Not only would this conflict with God's command against sex outside of marriage on the earthly level, but it would also conflict with the picture Paul presents on a spiritual level of presenting a faithful virgin to Christ: "I feel a divine jealousy for you, since I betrothed you to one husband, to present you as a pure virgin to Christ" (2 Corinthians 11:2). Just as a fiancé would be devastated to hear that his betrothed had been sleeping around, so is our ultimate Bridegroom devastated when He sees us following false teachers, who pollute the purity of our faith.

Let's jump ahead in the Song for a moment to see that the maiden is indeed remaining pure. It is not until Song of Songs 4 that the bridegroom addresses her as his bride and when, finally, the garden is unlocked. We read that she has been "a garden locked, a fountain sealed" until the wedding night:

A garden locked is my sister, my bride,
> a spring locked, a fountain sealed.
—Song 4:12

But then a few verses later, consummation and satisfaction happen, as the bridegroom refers to her as

a garden fountain, a well of living water,
> and flowing streams from Lebanon.
—Song 4:15

We remember that the Song is poetry and that the refrain that opens the Song and repeats throughout is the refrain of desire rather than a chronological telling of events.

It is also helpful to understand Near Eastern love poetry. In Song 2:5, in the midst of what seems like a description of physical intimacy, the woman says, "I am sick with love." According to Michael V. Fox, an expert in this genre of poetry, in ancient Near Eastern love poetry, people are never lovesick in the presence of their beloveds, only in their absence.[10]

The Shulammite longs for the day when the king will return and bring her into his chambers, just as we long for the day when we will be with Christ, when we will know as we have been known.

I think of the Christian refugees in Syria today—how they have lost everything in order to hold on to their faith. Because they would not deny Christ when ISIS militants told them to, they have lost their country, their homes, their families. Often they put their precious children in rickety boats, praying, as they watch them go, that they will make it across the choppy sea to safety. Do they not long for the return of the King, when He will make all things right? Then there will be no more sorrow, no more sin, no more sickness, and no more heartbreaking partings. The refugees, too, are "sick with love" as they wait for that beautiful day.

The love of longing for Christ is no ordinary love. It is a love that creates in us a desire for more and more of our Lover.

Lesson 3: Song of Songs 1:2–4

 Icebreaker

Describe a kiss that meant something to you, either on an earthly or spiritual level.

 Memory Work

1. Over the course of the rest of the study, you'll be memorizing Song of Songs 2:10–17. Because it's easier to memorize whole thoughts, every few weeks you'll be memorizing new verses and reviewing the previous verses. (In the back of this book, you will find the whole passage from the English Standard Version so the entire group can memorize the same words.) For this week, write out Song 2:10–11 on a card and memorize it immediately. Then keep the card visible during the week—take it with you while you walk or drive, put it on your bathroom mirror, tape it to your computer monitor—and keep rereading it. Frequent reviewing is the secret.

2. In the group, turn to the woman next to you and recite Song of Songs 2:10–11. Share with her any thoughts you have on that passage.

 Read Chapter 3 of *He Calls You Beautiful*

1. What insight did you gain by looking into the Song?

2. What stood out to you in this chapter and why?

*3. Read out loud Song 1:2–4. What quickens you from the reading and why?

*4. Instead of the Song beginning with the king first meeting the peasant woman, it begins with a refrain of desire that will repeat, with variations, throughout the Song. Why *this* refrain? What does this have to do with Christianity?

5. How is this refrain of desire echoed from the shepherd-king in Song of Songs 2:10–11? Is the idea that God desires intimacy with you something new to you? What does that mean to you? How is this different from the teaching of other religions?

6. When you look at your own heart, do you see passion for the Lord? If not, was there a time you did? What were you like then, and how have you changed?

7. A kiss from the King is when God brings you life from His Word or perhaps an answer to prayer or circumstances, showing He is mindful of you. How has God kissed you recently?

8. What kind of kisses does the Shulammite woman ask for?

*9. Read Numbers 12:1–9. Describe the disagreement and how God settled it.
   How did God say He spoke to Moses? With this in mind, what might a kiss
   on the mouth represent?

10. Minister and Bible commentary writer Matthew Henry talks about the
    gospel kiss, when we are awakened from our death sleep to Christ. Have
    you been awakened to Christ? What or who did God use to awaken you?

11. What does the woman say is better than wine? What does this mean? Can
    you relate to it? If so, explain.

12. What bells does the picture of "anointing oils" ring in your mind and spirit?
    (If you need help, see Psalm 23:5; Psalm 133:1–2; Exodus 40:9.)

*13. What is it about the *name* of Jesus that is like "oil poured out"?

*14. Who else loves the king besides the maiden (see Song 1:3–4)? What insight does this give you into the Song?

15. How does your sisters' love for Jesus (here in this group or elsewhere) strengthen your own love for Him? Be specific as to what helps you.

16. What is your takeaway from this week and why?

⤴ Prayer Time

Divide into clusters, share your requests, and then have the facilitator lead you in a time of thanksgiving and supplication. Keep the requests personal, if possible, rather than for people your group does not know.

Dark, but Lovely

The Gospel According to the Song of Songs

Don't advertise your beautiful faith without advertising your broken-down faults—because those broken-down faults are the exact reason why you need your beautiful faith.

—Ann Voskamp

*I*n the dance scene from *The Scent of a Woman,* Al Pacino plays a blind gentleman, Frank, who leads a woman in a tango that melts my heart. The shy and lovely Gabrielle Anwar plays Donna, who is hesitant when, in an elegant hotel dining room, Frank asks her,

"Would you like to learn to tango, Donna?"

"Right now?"

"I'm offering you my services, free of charge. What do you say?"

"Ah . . . I think I'd be a little afraid."

"Of what?"

"Afraid of making a mistake."

"No mistakes in the tango, Donna—not like life. That's what makes the tango so great. You make a mistake, get all tangled up, you just tango on."

He is wooing. "Why don't you try? Will you try it?"

A long pause.

Finally, a shy smile; then she agrees to give it a try.

He has wooed her. Now he must win her. He takes her hand and leads her to the dance floor. She is tentative, scared, and self-conscious. He places her hand on his shoulder and his hand on the small of her back. The music begins. He leads, at first gently, but then he pivots her quickly away from him and back as she laughs in delight. She is relaxing, trusting him now to lead her into adventure. What follows is a dance of enthralling grace and passion.[1]

This is how it is with the Lord. In the beginning we are shy, uncertain. But He gently woos, leading us to the dance floor. As we see how capable He is, we begin to relax; then we begin to dance!

We see both this shyness and curiosity in the words of the Shulammite woman:

> I am very dark, but lovely,
>> O daughters of Jerusalem,
> like the tents of Kedar,
>> like the curtains of Solomon.
> —Song 1:5

On an earthly level, this is a Cinderella story. This young woman is oppressed, not by her stepsisters but by her stepbrothers. (She doesn't call them her brothers but rather her "mother's sons," indicating they are likely her stepbrothers.) Working all day under the scorching sun, her skin has become weathered, in contrast to the protected skin of the wealthy women of the city, the daughters of Jerusalem. And yet, despite this sense of being less than, she is already hearing the faint melody of love. There is a dream in her heart, a dream that her oppressive stepbrothers would no doubt ridicule. For how could a king choose their sweaty, sticky, sunburned stepsister to be his bride?

The scene is set for this shepherd-king to ride in on his white horse. It is not one of the daughters of Jerusalem he chooses but her! He gazes at her longingly. What she dreamed of is happening, but now she is all the more self-conscious. She feels the need to explain why her skin is dark and her own vineyard (meaning herself) is unkempt:

> Do not gaze at me because I am dark,
>> because the sun has looked upon me.

My mother's sons were angry with me;
>   they made me keeper of the vineyards,
>   but my own vineyard I have not kept!
—Song 1:6

Despite her self-consciousness, she is drawn to him. She longs to see him again and asks how she can find him. She is told to "follow in the tracks of the flock" (Song 1:8), and when she finds him, he tells her how beautiful she is. The romance has begun.

Both Dark and Lovely

"Dark, but lovely" is such a good phrase for the two parts of the gospel, for we are both dark and lovely. We are so sinful that Christ had to go to the cross for us, yet we are so loved that He did. In the beginning of our relationship with Him, we are often very aware of our unworthiness, of being as dark as "the tents of Kedar." (The tents belonged to a nomadic tribe associated with Ishmael, who was outside the presence of God.) And yet, despite our feelings of unworthiness, we have a faint song in our hearts. From where did that come?

This is how Brent Curtis and John Eldredge put it in *The Sacred Romance:* "Someone or something has romanced us from the beginning with creek-side singers and pastel sunsets, with the austere majesty of snowcapped mountains and the poignant flames of autumn colors telling us of something—or someone—leaving, with a promise to return."[2]

There is a great King who loves us and has the power to make us as beautiful as the curtains of Solomon. The only curtain in Solomon's temple was next to the holy of holies, next to the presence of God (see Exodus 26:33; 2 Chronicles 3:14). Because of Christ's sacrificial love, it is possible for us to come near to a holy God without fear.

And so the gospel is our own Cinderella story. Because of our sin nature, we are as dark as the tents of Kedar: far from the presence of God. Yet, because of Christ, we can be made as lovely as the curtains of Solomon: cleansed and invited into the presence of a holy God.

And how God loves to woo us into His presence! He is always the One who initiates the dance. We may think it is we who choose Him, but we could not, for we are too dark, too depraved, to choose Him. We were dead in our sins, and a dead person cannot do anything. So let us abandon the pride that makes us think that because we are smarter or more sensitive than the average person, we somehow choose God. Instead, He reaches down into the deep waters and draws out our lifeless bodies, breathes life into us, and then irresistibly woos us into the dance.

For each of us, this wooing, this invitation to the dance, is different. Some respond quite quickly, while others take a long time. Before the foundation of the world, His Spirit was hovering over each person who would be His—who one day would respond to His invitation to the dance.

We may not have been aware of His Spirit hovering over us, yet when we look back on our lives, we can see His work. Lauren Winner puts it like this: "Sometimes, as in a great novel, you cannot see until you get to the end that God was leaving clues for you all along. Sometimes you wonder, *How did I miss it? Surely any idiot should have been able to see from the second chapter that it was Miss Scarlet in the conservatory with the rope.*"[3]

How did He awaken you? Recording artist Sara Groves sings of a young woman lying on her back in the grass, looking up at the stars, wondering if there is a loving God.[4] I had a fifth-grade schoolteacher—Miss Kolander—who loved Jesus. I never forgot her kindness or how radiant she became when she talked about Jesus.

I sometimes sense when God's Spirit is hovering over someone, wooing her. I tentatively say something about what Jesus is doing in my life, and she lights up, telling me of a sister or a neighbor who has been telling her of Jesus. I can almost feel the wind come up, like when I'm sitting becalmed in a sailboat and suddenly I feel the breeze and scurry to lift the sail. I did not make the wind and have no power over it, but oh, if I can catch it, we are in for a ride!

That's how I felt with Debbie. My friend Twila and I play pickleball (a less strenuous form of tennis) regularly at the YMCA as a way to meet and love non-Christians. That's where Twila first met Debbie. Twila invited Debbie to a musical night at her home, where various friends sang or played an instrument and I shared a brief testimony of how Christ was changing my life.

Debbie came that evening; then a few weeks later, she came all by herself to a retreat I was giving locally. It is hard to go alone somewhere, but Debbie was being irresistibly drawn. She was following "the tracks of the flock" (Song 1:8), yearning to find the Shepherd we had found.

At the end of the retreat, she came to me shyly and asked, "Why can't I stop crying when you speak?"

I paused. "I think God is wooing you to Himself."

She teared up again.

Twila and I then invited a few of the other women we'd met at pickleball, including Debbie, to a seeker study—a short gospel study of Jesus.[5] The first time Debbie came to the study, I could tell she was still in the darkness of the womb, suffering from the contractions that had begun to upset her life. I believed she was close, though, to being thrust into the light and a whole new exciting world.

We were studying the gospel of John, and Debbie lamented, "My head hurts. I can't understand how Jesus has always been—I thought He began at Christmas." She said she drove home with a headache from thinking so hard! I thought, *Oh, Lord, bring her out of the birth canal!*

Her husband, Ron, was waiting for her at the door. He said, "Did you figure out how Jesus could always have been?" (His curiosity was evidence that he too was being awakened.)

She said, "I'm still trying to wrap my head around that."

The next week I invited Debbie and Ron to dinner, along with another Christian couple. Ron is a big, burly man who worked for FEMA, the disaster-relief arm of the US government. At one point when we were clearing dishes, Ron leaned over the counter, looked me in the eyes, and spoke sternly: "What you have been teaching my wife is *not* what I've heard in church all my life."

We all froze momentarily, for the wind had come up. I lifted the sail, asking, "How is it different, Ron?"

"You told her that to go to heaven, she doesn't have to do anything other than trust what Jesus did at the cross."

"Yes, that's true."

"Are you telling me she doesn't have to be *good*?"

My heart was overwhelmed with compassion for Ron and anger at those who preach a different gospel, which is really no gospel at all. Ron and Debbie had been churchgoers, but they had not been rescued by the Savior. Spontaneously I leaned over the counter, covering Ron's tightly grasped hands with mine.

"Oh Ron! We don't have to earn our way—Jesus did it for us."

His eyes grew moist. *Could it be?* Then the struggle: "But that's too easy."

"That's why it is called *amazing* grace."

His brow furrowed. This was not what he had been taught. That day with Ron and Debbie, I showed them a list from Tim Keller's *Gospel in Life* that contrasts religion with the gospel. The first on the list was this: under religion we say, "I obey; therefore, I'm accepted," while under the gospel we say, "I'm accepted; therefore, I obey."[6]

Ron kept reading through the list, and then in a whisper that moved us all, he said, "I guess I'm religious."

His sail was catching the wind.

A Slow and Widening Light

That day in the kitchen, when the wind came up, Debbie pondered aloud, "I think if this happens to me, it will happen gradually."

"Or it might happen suddenly," one of my friends said. "God knocked Saul to the ground."

"But can't it happen slowly?" Debbie asked.

"Yes," I said. "For some it is a slow and widening light. It might be like driving from Nebraska to Colorado. You might not know when you crossed the border, but there comes a moment when you look at the snowcapped peaks and think, *I'm not in Nebraska anymore.*

A week later Debbie texted me, "3:00 p.m. South of Egg Harbor. I get it. I don't have to do anything, do I?"

The next time I was with Debbie, I could see she had traveled beyond Nebraska and into the light—into the breathtaking mountains of Colorado. And, oh, she was excited, eager to tell others, just as the Shulammite woman had a contagious excitement that made others fall in love with the bridegroom.

In Song 1:4, these "others" (or your Bible might say "friends" or "daughters of Jerusalem") are first introduced. Although it might seem strange to have others suddenly singing in the midst of such an intimate scene, remember, this is not prose but a poetic song. This is the language of public worship and, as Dr. Ellen F. Davis says, shows "an 'evangelical' dimension to the Song. This celebration of love is intensely personal yet also, paradoxically, a public event, in which this woman gladly shares with 'the maidens' (verse 3) her rejoicing in 'the king.'"[7] The maidens echo her excitement about this shepherd-king, for the *you* in the following verse in Hebrew is masculine singular:

> We will exult and rejoice in you;
>> we will extol your love more than wine.
>
> —Song 1:4

Debbie began bringing her neighbors to Bible study. I knew that Ron was close to faith as well, for he had so many questions. The fragrance of Christ in Debbie was wooing him. Ron is not exactly sure *when* he crossed the border from unbelief to belief. Was it when he began reading *The Prodigal God* by Tim Keller? Was it when his mother died and he couldn't stop thinking about eternity? Was it after he texted me, "How can I know whether I am a Christian or not?" But one day, while Ron listened to praise music in the car, God's Spirit witnessed to his spirit that he was His child. Ron and Debbie were baptized together in the waters of Green Bay at my cottage. What a joyful celebration!

This is one way spiritual marriage differs from earthly marriage. In earthly marriage, we want to be the only one to intimately know our beloved, but in spiritual marriage, we are eager for others to know Him. This is why the bride in the Song is portrayed both individually and corporately. We see this in the bride's eagerness for the virgins to know and love the bridegroom. This would not happen in an earthly marriage! But this is what happens when we fall in love with Jesus: because He is so wonderful and the gospel is such good news, we cannot help but tell others.

In the Song, we see a repetition of "you whom my soul loves." It appears the first time here:

> Tell me, you whom my soul loves,
>> where you pasture your flock,
>> where you make it lie down at noon.
>
> —Song 1:7

Ancient Israel shared Scripture orally, not on the printed page as we do. Instead of reading these words, they *heard* these phrases repeated throughout the Song. Those words reminded them of other passages in Scripture, just like a popular advertising slogan we hear again and again reminds us of the whole ad. The phrase "You whom my soul loves" brought to mind the Shema, which they prayed morning and night: "Hear, O Israel: The LORD our God, the LORD is one. You shall love the LORD your God will all your heart and with all your soul and with all your might" (Deuteronomy 6:4–5).

And then when the Song goes on to say, "where you pasture your flock, where you make it lie down at noon," would it not ring bells of the Twenty-Third Psalm? As Dr. Ellen Davis says, "The fact that this beloved-of-the-soul is a shepherd further reinforces his identification with God."[8]

And so in the Song, we see the power of poetry and repetition helping us understand more fully God's great love for us—and quickening in us a desire to tell others about the joy we have found!

"JESUS, HELP ME!"

As I have watched Debbie and Ron, who had been married nearly fifty years when they came to Christ, I am amazed at the transformation I see happening. Though I *know* that Jesus is real, it's almost like being born again all over again myself when I see new life emerge in others.

Ron is a veteran of the Vietnam War, which left the souls of so many men wounded. Ever since his time in Vietnam, Ron has suffered from tendencies toward verbal abuse. He loves Debbie, yet he would still habitually fly off the handle, wounding her. After all these years, could Ron possibly be rescued from the power sin had over him? Could he be untied and divorced, as poet John Donne put it, from the Enemy?

One night Ron and Debbie took me out to dinner at a delightful garden restaurant in Door County, Wisconsin, called the Summer Kitchen. I was in the backseat, and Ron was driving, with Debbie in the passenger seat. When we got close to the restaurant, Debbie said, "Ron, turn at the next left."

"I know where to turn."

"Don't be so touchy!"

"Don't be so bossy!"

Then Ron turned so sharply that the tires screeched and my purse flew to the floor, spilling its contents.

"Hey, hey, hey!" I cried.

"Sorry, Dee," Ron said abjectly.

He turned off the car, and we sat there for a moment in silence.

"Listen," I said softly, "you're Christians now. You just can't talk to each other like this."

Ron swiveled his big neck to look at me, furrowing his bushy eyebrows. "Why not?"

"I'll show you when we get in the restaurant."

Inside, seated at a table overlooking a little garden of Queen Anne's lace and blue cornflowers, I pulled out my Bible and opened it to Ephesians 4, explaining that Paul is telling the church in Ephesus to put off their old way of life and to put on their new way of life in Christ. "Each time, he tells them to stop a bad old way by replacing it with the new way in Christ. He tells the thief to stop stealing and to start working for a living. And when it comes to how we talk to one another, he says, 'Let all bitterness and wrath and anger and clamor and slander be put away from you, along with all malice. Be kind to one another, tenderhearted, forgiving one another, as God in Christ forgave you' (Ephesians 4:31–32)."

Ron furrowed his brows again, pondering.

The next day, alone at home, Debbie and Ron started quarreling again. Debbie said, "Wait, wait, wait! Let's read that Ephesians thing." And so they did, aloud.

Ron said, "That sounds great, Debbie, but I can't do it!"

Then that big beautiful man grabbed his Bible, ran out into the woods, fell on his knees, and cried out with tears, "Jesus, help me do it!"

It still takes my breath away to see how gentled Ron has become. He testifies openly of the power of His Savior. "For years I tried to change, but I couldn't do it. I needed Jesus to do it in me."

Ron has been ravished by the love of Christ.

THANKS BE TO GOD

We are all like Ron in that we may know *what* to do, but we can't do it! We cry with Paul, "Wretched man that I am! Who will deliver me from this body of death?" (Romans 7:24).

The answer? "Thanks be to God through Jesus Christ our Lord!" (Romans 7:25).

The gospel can deliver the unbeliever from the penalty of sin, but it can also deliver the believer from the power of sin. We must remember, each day, that we are "dark, but lovely" (Song 1:5). This is the gospel: the bad news of our sin nature yet the good news of His love and His blood continually cleansing us as we repent and turn from repeated sins.

Our youngest daughter, Annie, is an excellent, caring nurse. One day a doctor pressured her to do a procedure that she wasn't sure she understood. Though she at first protested, she then gave in to the pressure. Immediately afterward, she realized she had not done the procedure correctly. *Why did I do that and put the patient at risk?* She knew it was because of her heart idol of approval—she had wanted the doctor's approval more than God's approval. So she repented and knew she had to also go and confess to the bad-tempered doctor. Indeed, he swore and yelled at her, but Annie stood there and took it. When he calmed down, she sincerely apologized. Then she confessed to the patient, and another nurse helped Anne redo the procedure correctly.

I knew it was the gospel, "the dark, but lovely," that rescued Annie in that situation. She acknowledged the darkness in her heart, owning her sin. She calmly withstood the rage of an out-of-control doctor because she knew she was lovely, beloved in the sight of God, and on that rock she stood while the waters roared.

Philosopher and statesman Thomas Moore explains, "The person who cannot admit that he is wrong is desperately insecure. At root he does not feel accepted."[9]

When we know we are accepted, we are willing to admit that we cannot live the Christian life in our own strength. We are desperate creatures who need the Spirit of the living God to rescue us not only from the penalty of sin but also from its daunting power. We must cry, cry, cry out for the One our soul loves.

As we see in the Song, it is the deeper picture of Jesus Christ that has the power to deliver us. As we see how loved we are, our hearts of stone begin to melt into hearts of flesh. We begin to trust His love enough to turn from our idols and run instead to Him. It is then we find, to our astonishment, that *He* is delivering us, making us better wives, husbands, parents, and people.

So let us cooperate with God's process by realizing how deeply loved we are by the One who sees us naked, with every blemish, yet loves us to the sky.

Lesson 4: Song of Songs 1:5–8

 Icebreaker

In this last week, was there a time when you felt God's presence? If so, share when and why.

 Memory Work

Review Song of Songs 2:10–11 every day.

 Listen

Before you begin this study on your own, prepare your heart by listening to Matt Redman's "Nothing but the Blood."[10]

 Read Chapter 4 of *He Calls You Beautiful*

1. What insight did you gain by looking into the Song of Songs?

2. What stood out to you in this chapter and why?

3. Read aloud Song 1:4–8 and share anything that is meaningful to you and why.

4. Read Song 1:4. The "others" mentioned are a chorus of maidens who are also drawn to the bridegroom. God uses three metaphors to describe His people:

the body, the building, and the bride. Each has an individual and a corporate aspect. Find both (individual and corporate) in the following:

a. The body (see 1 Corinthians 12:12–20)

b. The building (see Ephesians 2:19–20)

c. The bride (see Song 1:4)

5. Read Song 1:5.

a. The tents of Kedar not only were dirty and weathered but also represented those cut off from the presence of the Lord. What emotions do you see expressed in Psalm 120:5–7? What is the maiden saying about herself?

b. The curtains of Solomon had the opposite connotation (see Exodus 26:33) of the tents of Kedar. What do you think these curtains represent and why? What is she saying about herself here?

*c. How is it possible for a child of God to be both dark and lovely at once?

6. In the verse we read, the word *dark* doesn't represent just one thing but has many connotations. What can you discover from the following verses about why we might be feeling dark?

   a. Psalm 143:3

   b. Proverbs 4:19

   c. Isaiah 5:20

7. Read Song 1:6.

   a. What do you think the bride is feeling and why?

b. How do you know she is uncomfortable with the shepherd-king's attention?

c. Compare this with Peter's reaction to Jesus in Luke 5:8. What insight does the comparison give you?

*d. Have you ever felt like this in the presence of holiness? If so, share specifics.

8. In Song 1:15, how does the bridegroom reassure her? (See also Song 4:7.)

9. Compare this to Isaiah 1:18. How is it possible to be made this clean? (If you need help, see 2 Corinthians 5:17–18.)

*10. An awareness of our dual natures—the deceitfulness of our sinful hearts, yet the fact that we are cleansed and loved—can help us have the faith to repent. Share a recent time when you've messed up and how understanding this dual nature might have helped you.

11. In Song 1:7, how can you see the Shema (see Deuteronomy 6:4–5) again?

12. In Song 1:8, how is the bride told to find her beloved? What part did other Christians play in leading you to find the Good Shepherd?

13. What is your takeaway or application for this week?

 Prayer Time

Divide into smaller groups. Share with the others an area where you keep stumbling, and then ask for their prayer. Or share a need in your life.

The Apple Tree and the Lily

Cultivating Intimacy with God

How do I love thee? Let me count the ways.

—Elizabeth Barrett Browning

In 1932, my father noticed a strikingly beautiful woman in his English class at Northwestern University. Detective work helped him discover her name and phone number, and he called her at home.

"Hello, Marianne. My name is Bob Brown and I am in your English class. I am the man who wears the Northwestern University sweater. I'd like very much to invite you to dinner."

"Thank you, Bob. I'll have to ask my mother. I'll be right back."

There were two young men wearing Northwestern U sweaters in my mother's English class, but she only remembered one: a homely, awkward young man. Mother covered the receiver, waited a moment, and then said, "I'm so sorry, Bob, but my mother says I may not go."

The next day in class, Mother saw another man wearing a Northwestern U sweater: an extremely handsome honor student. She inquired of her friends and discovered indeed that was Bob Brown.

She walked over to him and said, "I'm so happy to tell you that my mother has reconsidered and I may go."

My father always called my mother "sweetheart" or "darling" and was absolutely smitten with her all of his life. When she sang solos in church, tears ran down his cheeks. For sixty-five years of marriage, every day he told her, "You are the best thing that ever happened to me." When my father died, my mother missed those continual expressions of his love, though every day when she sat at the piano he had given her, she saw his engraved plaque from Elizabeth Barrett Browning's poem: "How do I love thee? Let me count the ways."

LET ME COUNT THE WAYS

Throughout the Song, the bridegroom keeps praising his bride, using various terms of endearment. The endearment in Song 1:9 ("my darling," NIV) and 1:15 ("my love") is the Hebrew *rayah*, which means "friend" or "companion" but also has the connotation of "lover." It is literally like "the French *petite amie*, 'sweetheart,' which is literally 'little friend.' "[1] She is all of these to him: lover, friend, companion, and sweetheart.

What is interesting about the bridegroom's praise is that we never really know what the woman looks like, but we do know how he feels about her—and we know that she has great strength of character. She is as powerful and majestic as a galloping horse, as peaceable and gentle as a dove, and as outstanding "as a lily among brambles" (Song 2:2). It is amazing to her that she could captivate one so wonderful (a king!), but as he keeps praising her, she opens, like a flower to the sun. And now she begins to praise him, counting the ways in return.

> While the king was on his couch,
>   my nard gave forth its fragrance.
> My beloved is to me a sachet of myrrh
>   that lies between my breasts.
>   —Song 1:12–13

She calls him a king yet also her beloved, images of *dôd* again, the boiling pot. She likens herself to the wildflower (the spikenard) that, when opening, gives forth the intense sweet aroma of nard, the same perfume that Mary of Bethany used to anoint Jesus. She compares him to a sachet of myrrh, a powerful allusion to Christ. Myrrh is extracted by repeatedly piercing the tree's heartwood and allowing the gum to trickle out and harden into bitter, aromatic red droplets called tears. Later in the Song, the bridegroom tells her,

> I will go away to the mountain of myrrh
>   and the hill of frankincense.
>   —Song 4:6

Our Savior went to the "mountain of myrrh" to be pierced repeatedly, and His blood flowed so that we might be washed of our sin. In fact, throughout the Song, the bridegroom is associated with gold, frankincense, and myrrh. (You see all three together in the wedding scene.) This is the One the Magi worshiped, the One born to lay down His life for His bride. She cannot help but respond to such passionate love. Here is the dance again, with the bridegroom initiating and the beloved responding.

I was reminded of this dance in the most unlikely place recently: a car dealership. Now that I am a widow, I often ask God to be my husband when I walk into situations in which I could easily be taken advantage of, such as buying a car. I hold to God's promise that He will care for widows and orphans (see Psalm 68:5).

When I first arrived at the Subaru dealership, I was a bit uncomfortable with the salesman. *Not him, Lord!* And just minutes later, he received a call and had to leave! A young man named David came to the rescue. He was kind, gentle, and not at all pushy. Somewhere in our conversation David used the word *blessing,* and I quickened, thinking this might mean God was bending down and answering my prayer.

"Blessing!" I said. "That's an interesting word choice, David."

He smiled and said, "I am a Christian."

"And what does the word *Christian* mean to you?"

Now he outright laughed, for he knew exactly what I was trying to discern. Indeed, he made it clear he belonged to the Lord. With joy, we grinned at one another, shook hands with gusto, reveling in the realization that we were family! Our conversation then went much deeper, as it can with fellow believers, and we discovered we had been enriched by courses at Covenant Seminary. When he asked me what I was writing, I found, quite to my astonishment, that he delighted in the picture of Christ and His bride in the Song. *Really, Lord? For a young man to see this is quite rare! You are kissing me, providing for me, giving me far more than I even asked for!*

Then I discovered that David was a professional ballroom dancer. He and his new bride were teaching couples at their church how to dance. He told me, "There is such a parallel between dancing and our relationship with Christ. The man leads, but his purpose is to make the woman look beautiful, just as Christ does with His bride."

I thought, *That is exactly what we see in the Song.* He lavishes love on her, he calls her to follow him, and when she surrenders, she is the beautiful bride who is "coming up from the wilderness, leaning on her beloved" (Song 8:5).

David and I both sensed the Lord's presence in our encounter. Not only did I buy a car, but I was also then invited to give a retreat at his church. The theme? "Responding to the Lord of the Dance"! David and his wife, Rhondalay, danced for us—a poignant dance to "Be Thou My Vision." It was such a picture of two being more beautiful together than either could be alone (see Proverbs 30:18–19). And as David led with strength, twirling and dipping Rhondalay, and as she responded with joyful trust, blossoming, I was reminded of the apple tree and the lily (see Song 2:2–3).

UNDISTRACTED DEVOTION

As the bridegroom continues to woo his beloved, she is so overcome that she can't stop staring at him. In fact, he tells her she has "dove's eyes."

The dove is known for her gentleness and is often used as a symbol of peace. Doves are also monogamous: chaste and faithful to their mates. Doves also coo to one another, as these two in the Song are certainly doing. But as these allusions to the dove come to mind, we have to ask, What is the significance of him telling her she has doves' *eyes*? The dove's enormous eyes are wide set and have no peripheral vision—she is focused on what is straight ahead of her.

My dear friend Linda Strom has been a mentor to me, bringing me into a prison ministry that takes my breath away, for we have seen God move so mightily. Both Linda and I were blessed with amazing husbands, and both of us lost our husbands to cancer when we thought we would have them much longer.

Linda told me a story recently that is quite personal, yet this dear widow gladly gave me permission to share it. It penetrates my heart, and I pray it will yours as well.

We sat at her kitchen table, steaming mugs of coffee in our hands, lingering over the Song. Linda looked at me, with moist eyes, and said, "That He would love me like *this*."

"I know."

She took a sip of her coffee and closed her eyes. "There were times in lovemaking with Dallas when I was preoccupied and distracted, my mind racing to the prison ministry. Dallas would suddenly be still and whisper in his deep voice, 'Where are you?'"

She opened her eyes and I saw tears.

I nodded. I too felt regret about moments missed with Steve, now irretrievable. How could I have been so preoccupied with lesser things when my husband was longing to connect with me?

Linda continued. "I can do the same thing with the Lord. I'm going through the motions, reading the Bible—but I'm not there. My mind is far away. And He whispers, 'Where are you?'"

Here, in the newness of love, the Shulammite woman is *not* distracted, for she has dove's eyes. She moves closer and closer to him. She tells him,

Behold, you are beautiful, my beloved, truly delightful.
Our couch is green;
   the beams of our house are cedar;
   our rafters are pine.
—Song 1:16–17

She is fantasizing about the day when they will be wed, when she will move from the house of her mother to live with him in his home. He will make love to her in his fragrant chambers of cedar and pine, woods rich in Israel's tradition and which Solomon used in building the temple and other buildings (see 1 Kings 6:15–18; 7:2–3, 7).

I am so blessed to live in a cabin that my loving parents passed on to me; it's tucked away in a forest of cedars by the lapping waters of Green Bay. Come June, I can open all my windows and let the fragrance of cedar waft in. It's a taste of the Garden of Eden and of the scene painted in the Song. Smell, sight, touch. A promise of heaven to come. A reminder of the time when I will look to Him alone.

A BEAUTIFUL OTHERNESS

In this continuing passionate dialogue, the bridegroom compares his love to a wildflower:

> As a lily among brambles,
>> so is my love among the young women.
> —Song 2:2

And she responds:

> As an apple tree among the trees of the forest,
>> so is my beloved among the young men.
> —Song 2:3

Though Christianity, in contrast to other world religions, clearly states that men and women are equal in God's sight (see Galatians 3:28), it is also clear that God created men and women differently. Men are called to protect, like an "apple tree" provides sustenance and shade. Women are called to provide fragrance and beauty, a gentleness that changes the atmosphere, like "a lily among brambles."

What caused Adam to be so pleased when God brought Eve to him? First, he was thrilled to realize that *finally* here was someone *like* him. He had been lonely, a loneliness augmented by having named all the animals but seeing no one like him—no one with whom he could fellowship.

Richard Mouw, former president of Fuller Theological Seminary, quipped, "That was kind of like spending the whole day, wishing you had a date, in the Bronx Zoo."[2] But now God puts Adam into a deep sleep, pierces his side, and creates a woman from the man's rib. When God brings the *first* bride to the *first* bridegroom, Adam breaks out into the *first* song:

This at last is bone of my bones
> and flesh of my flesh;
she shall be called Woman,
> because she was taken out of Man.
> —Genesis 2:23

Adam recognizes that finally here is someone like him—yet she is so other. Author Mike Mason says, "The whole thing begins with a wondrous *looking*, a helpless staring, an irresistible compulsion simply to behold."[3]

Our world has not treasured the beauty of otherness between men and women, and the fallout is great. One result of disregarding the differences between men and women is that men are often hesitant to be gallant for fear of being offensive. We see this in even small ways. For example, I used to almost always receive an offer of help to put my suitcase in the overhead bin when getting on a plane. Today I often struggle alone. I'm only five feet tall, so I have to place it on my head, stand on tip-toe, and push upward. Then, when we're unloading, I have to stand on the seat to get my bag down. If a man does jump up to help, I am *so* grateful and thank him profusely and loudly!

Speaker Paige Benton Brown tells of going with her college friends to see *The Last of the Mohicans* and "gorgeous" Daniel Day-Lewis. In this movie, the men died to protect their maidens. As the women left the movie in a dreamy daze, Paige's friend fell on her knees in the parking lot and cried, "But where are the Mohicans!?"

They still exist—and they are generally men who are sensitive to God's Spirit.

A year ago a frightening storm came over the bay where I live in Door County, Wisconsin, and it took all my strength to close my windows against its rising fury. Then I heard the cedars cracking, falling, thundering against the ground and my house. I thought of these words: "The voice of the LORD breaks the cedars" (Psalm 29:5).

In the eerie silence that followed, I walked out to see enormous destruction in the yard, with sixteen tall cedars down. The gigantic swing set my son had built was destroyed, and my lawn had disappeared under all the cedars. I knelt and thanked God that the house stood firm and that I was not hurt. Yet still, it was overwhelming to see such destruction. I cried, "Lord, please be my husband!"

In the next hour, three different Christian men (Dennis, Mark, and Jonathan) drove down to check on me, and Jonathan spent the next week cleaning up my yard. My friend Vicki quipped, "That was three husbands! Polygamy!" No, that was the Mohicans! They were being the apple trees God called them to be: protecting and providing.

Likewise, instead of suppressing our femininity, we as women must value how much our cold and impersonal world needs our relational gifts. The Swiss physician Paul Tournier talked about how his wife, Nelly, could absolutely change the atmosphere at his medical meetings with caring questions. Tournier called it "a woman's sense of the person."[4] In the home, in the church, and in the workplace, we need women to exercise that sense of the person, being alert to needs and drawing out the deep waters of others' souls. A woman in a small group can be a tremendous catalyst for the discussion if she exercises her relational gifts, asking shy members to elaborate, being alert to facial signs that someone might have something to say, and encouraging him or her to share. She also can welcome newcomers, inviting them right into her home, watering their souls with love. She can comfort the grieving, encourage the fainthearted, and play the hostess in conversation. How desperately we need women to exercise the feminine gifts that can cause a desert to bloom!

The flowers to which the Song compares her—a rose of Sharon and a lily of the valley—are wildflowers the prophets used as symbols of God's mercy to Israel after her devastation by enemies. Look at how similar this passage from Hosea is to passages we have already seen in the Song.[5]

I will love them freely. . . .
I will be like the dew to Israel;
    he shall blossom like the lily. . . .
They shall return and dwell beneath my shadow; . . .
They shall blossom like the vine.

    —Hosea 14:4–5, 7

God can work through His daughters to help His people blossom like the vine. He intentionally made us male and female, for there is a purpose in our unique gifting, in our otherness. Together the body of Christ represents the male and female sides of God, loving wholly, as He does.

One result of not appreciating the beauty of two who are other becoming one is the redefinition of marriage. There are many reasons God ordained marriage to be between one man and one woman, not between two men or two women. Only marriage between a man and a woman reflects the mystery of our union with the other, who is God. God's plan for marriage also stretches us to move out of our own depth and into the deep, mysterious waters of the opposite sex.

God's plan for marriage also increases our portfolios as individuals. Think of it like this: When you apply for a job, you might bring a portfolio, showing the range of employment experiences you have had. Varied experiences tend to increase wisdom in problem solving. In our marriage, Steve's maleness caused him to look at things differently than I did. Living with him immensely increased my portfolio for problem solving.

Soon after Steve died of cancer, I told my grief counselor, "Sometimes I wish I knew what Steve would have done—and then I realize, *I do know*, and it helps me make a better decision." When our youngest daughter's future husband came to me, asking permission to date her, I thought about how Steve would have responded with his strong desire to protect his daughter. I said, "David, I like you. And Steve would have loved you. But you own guns and a motorcycle, and Steve wouldn't have wanted Annie around either, so for now I must say no."

David said, "I'll sell them immediately."

Thinking about what Steve would have done expanded my portfolio and revealed David's heart. I said, "Well, David, then you may date her."

God's plan from the beginning was to bring two who were alike, *and yet so other*, together. Do you see how this points to the mystery of Christ and His bride?

Our God cherishes us so much that He humbled Himself to become like us, to be made flesh, identifying with us even to death, going down to the grave. He became like us so that He might rescue us. Because He became fully man, He can empathize with our temptations.

And yet He is the Other. He is perfect in holiness, resplendent in glory, and sacrificial in love. "In him," Colossians 1:17 tells us, "all things hold together." He is fully God. He is *so* Other that we can hardly grasp how One so glorious could love us—could indeed, as the Scripture tells us, delight in us (see Isaiah 62:4). Yet He does.

In Hosea, God says to His bride, "I will betroth you to me forever" (Hosea 2:19). "To know the Lord," Mike Mason writes, "is to be brought into a personal relationship so dramatic and overwhelming that marriage is only a pale image of it."[6]

It causes me to wonder, every day of my life, that the One who set the stars in place would lavish His love on me. And oh how my portfolio has expanded since His Spirit came to live in me! The *moment* we come into relationship with Him, He takes the blinders from our eyes and we see life differently. Transitory things become less important, and the grace we have received from God begins to flow to others. This is what it means to be born again, for His Spirit comes to live in us. The process of conforming us to His image continues as we spend time with Him, gazing on His beauty and becoming like the One we behold.

THE LEAST INADEQUATE METAPHOR

Jonathan Edwards was concerned when thousands were proclaiming Christ during the Great Awakening in the mid-1700s. Were they really being awakened? Edwards said famously, "There is a difference between having a rational judgment that honey is sweet, and having a sense of its sweetness."

You can recite the Apostles' Creed, agree with the great doctrines of the church, and even defend them to an unbeliever. But do you delight to sit under Christ's shadow, as Mary of Bethany did, hanging on His every word? Do you long for His presence?

This is why the metaphor of romantic love and sexual intimacy can turn the light on for what Jonathan Edwards called true religion. It's not enough to confess with our mouths; our *hearts* must be moved for God.

The next passage in the Song is so intimate it makes us blush. She is still fantasizing, for remember, the Hebrew word for "lovesick," or "faint with love," is used when the lover is absent. She is longing for him so much, in fact, that she is on the edge of delirium.

Sustain me with raisins;
>
> refresh me with apples,
>
> for I am sick with love.
>
His left hand is under my head,
>
> and his right hand embraces me!
>
> —Song 2:5–6

Dr. Ellen Davis says sexual love is the "least inadequate" metaphor for the love of Christ for His bride and her love for Him, the kind of love that we read in memoirs from saints of the past. They tell of such encounters with the living God that left them "faint."[7]

When Blaise Pascal died, a piece of parchment sewed into the lining of his coat was discovered. Apparently he had sewn it there so as to never forget what happened to him one night. It said,

> From about half-past ten in the evening until about half-past twelve . . .
>
> FIRE . . . God of Abraham, the God of Isaac, the God of Jacob, and
>
> not of the philosophers and savants. Certitude. Certitude. Feeling. Joy.
>
> Peace.[8]

Centuries later, on November 24, 1871, the great Chicago fire burned down D. L. Moody's church building. He went to New York in hopes of financial help and walked the streets praying in desperation. He tells what happened:

> One day, in the city of New York—oh, what a day!—I cannot describe it, I
>
> seldom refer to it; it is almost too sacred an experience to name. . . . I can
>
> only say that God revealed himself to me, and I had such an experience of
>
> his love that I had to ask him to stay his hand.[9]

Experiences like this are rare, and most of the time communion with God is like a quiet stream instead of a crashing wave—but it *can* be a crashing wave. So often the psalmist prays for intimacy with God, for a sense of His presence. He thirsts for intimacy with God, like a hunted deer *pants* for water. That is not to say we should seek emotional experiences. Instead, we should be seeking God, allowing His presence to make us thirst for Him even more.

God Is the One to Awaken Love

Perhaps it is an awareness of this danger of allowing emotions to take over that causes the Shulammite to speak words that will become a refrain of the Song:

I adjure you, O daughters of Jerusalem,
    by the gazelles or the wild does:
do not stir up or awaken love
    until it is ready!
—Song 2:7, NRSV

Some have interpreted these words as an admonition to the others not to awaken her loved one, who is sleeping in her arms. That could work on an earthly level except that we know that her lover is not actually with her yet. It also doesn't work on a spiritual level, for we have a God who never slumbers or sleeps. Also, the Hebrew word for "love" comes from a word meaning "affection," which indicates not a person but an emotion. So it seems an exhortation not to hurry love itself.

I remember my father telling me, "Never make momentous decisions precipitously." My mother was more specific: "You are married for a loooooooooong time, so get to know him and don't let him kiss you too soon."

When we were young, Steve and I heard Diana Ross and the Supremes in concert in Seattle. How I remember "You Can't Hurry Love"! The verses to the song are all about her longing, but the chorus is her mama's repeated warning, like the repeated warning from the Shulammite, not to move too fast.

Once awakened, sexual feelings often cloud a person's vision, causing him or her to leap into what turns out to be a very challenging marriage. Christian women in particular may feel guilty and marry out of shame a man with whom they have been intimate.

In speaking to the predominantly single congregation of New York's Redeemer Presbyterian Church, Neil Clark Warren, one of the founders of the online dating service eHarmony, explained the complex process that he and his son went through to come up with the twenty-nine variables that lead to strong marriages. They found that in almost all cases, if a couple had twenty-five or more of those variables match, they would have an excellent marriage. But what often happened, Warren said, is that the chemistry would take over and the couple would ask, "How many of those variables can we do without?"[10]

What does this repeated exhortation to not awaken love mean on a spiritual level? Are there dangers in methods that pressure young children to put their trust in Christ—or, for that matter, that pressure anyone to put his or her trust in Christ? And are we ever tempted to paint a romanticized picture of the Christian life in hopes of persuading our loved ones to surrender to Him?

I understand how deep our desire can be to see our loved ones come to faith in Christ. As a young believer, I sometimes became physically ill because I was so worried about my parents' salvation. I felt it was up to me, when it wasn't at all. I even wrote John Stott when my parents were taking Steve and me to England and said, "I think if my dad could just meet you, he might come to Christ."

Dr. Stott wrote me the kindest letter in reply, telling me he would have met with us if he were not in China, but he was confident that God was capable of bringing my dad to Christ. He encouraged me to trust God with my parents. It was the word I needed. I was able to surrender my parents to the Lord and see Him woo them each to Himself near the end of their lives.

In our desire to bring those we love to Christ, we may be tempted to paint a romanticized picture of the abundant life. Jesus turned around and told those following Him to count the cost. For though salvation is a free gift, the Christian life involves suffering, persecution, and sacrifice.

Those who come to Christ quickly or who have a romanticized view of the Christian life may be like the seed sown on rocky ground. Because they have no root, when troubles come, they fall away. This isn't what they expected at all! They didn't know the real Jesus. He doesn't always rescue us from the trouble of this world, though He does stand beside us and strengthen us.

It is comforting to remember that we are in relationship with God, who awakens us under the apple tree (see Song 8:5). We are to pray, to love, to be ready to give an answer for the hope within us, but we are not the ones who awaken others. We can actually quench the Spirit by trying to hurry love. We must not press our little children to say the Sinner's Prayer before they are ready; we must allow God to awaken their affections. In our zeal, we must not quarrel with unbelievers, confront them on Facebook, or manipulate them in any way. Those sinful actions may put a stumbling block in their path. Instead, we must move with His Spirit. Love, pray, and when you sense the wind coming up, be ready to lift the sail and share the hope that is within you. Work with the Spirit and not against Him.

Just as a husband and wife should work together in marriage, allowing their gifts to complement one another and keep from becoming lone rangers, so we must remember all through the day, whatever we are doing, that we are not on our own. The metaphor of marriage in the Song (as well as the metaphor of the vineyard— the vine and the branches) speaks of union and communion with Christ. The secret of a vital Christian life is union with Christ every moment, every day.

In order to work with God's Spirit, we must be able to recognize His voice. In the next scene in our love story, the Shulammite is thrilled to hear her shepherd-king's voice as he comes running to her.

LESSON 5: SONG OF SONGS 1:9–2:7

Icebreaker

During this past week, was there a time when you felt close to the Lord? If so, share when and why.

Memory Work

Add Song 2:12–13 to your memory work of Song 2:10–11. Write it out and memorize it right away. Then review 2:10–13 all week.

Listen

On your own, prepare your heart for this study by listening to Misty Edwards sing "Dove's Eyes."[11]

Read Chapter 5 of *He Calls You Beautiful*

1. What insight did you gain by looking into the Song?

2. What stood out to you in this chapter and why?

3. Read aloud Song 1:9–2:7. In this passage, they are praising each other, and she is also fantasizing about their wedding night. (The phrase "faint with

love" occurs in Hebrew poetry when the lover is absent.) What quickens you from this passage and why?

4. In each of the following passages, the king "counts the ways" his bride pleases him. How could each description refer to character as well as external beauty?

   a. Song 1:9 (see also Song 6:4)

   b. Song 1:15 (see also Matthew 10:16)

   c. Song 2:2 (see also Philippians 2:14–15)

5. Read Song 1:13. Myrrh is mentioned seven times in the Song and also with the birth and death of Christ. How was it used in John 19:39–40?

6. Has the truth of Christ's suffering and sacrifice sustained you in the trials of life? If so, share briefly.

7. To what does the groom compare his bride's eyes in 1:15, and what does this mean?

8. Review the story from Linda Strom in the chapter and comment. How you could better practice undistracted devotion when you are in the Word?

9. Read Song 2:1–4.

   a. How does the image of a lily suggest femininity? How can women, both single and married, enhance their world with these qualities?

b. How does the image of a shading apple suggest masculinity? How can men, both single and married, enhance their world with these qualities?

c. How might these differences between femininity and masculinity also be seen spiritually between Christ and His bride? (If you need help, Hosea 14:5–7 and 2 Corinthians 2:14 may give insight.)

*d. What happens to a culture that no longer cherishes the differences between the genders? To a marriage?

e. How might the Lord be speaking to you concerning this?

10. Being under the shadow or the covering of the Lord is a frequent metaphor in Scripture. The same Hebrew words are used in Psalm 57:1 (translated "refuge") and Isaiah 51:16 (translated "shadow"). Share a specific time when God protected you or was a refuge to you.

11. Read Song 2:7. What might this admonition mean on an earthly level? On a spiritual level, why is it better not to press children (or anyone) to receive Christ but simply to share the gospel and let His Spirit do the rest? How might you apply this?

12. Just as a husband or wife must learn to appreciate the differences of the opposite sex and work with his or her spouse, so must we learn to work with the Lord, taking His hand in the dance. Can you think of an example of how you have done this in your devotional time, in evangelism, or in any of the ways you serve Him?

13. What is your takeaway or application this week and why?

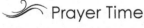 Prayer Time

Pray together to be less distracted in your time with the Lord. Have dove's eyes as you support each other in prayer.

Come Away, My Love!

Cleaving to Him Alone

Just as the woman in the Song quickened at hearing the
voice of her bridegroom, so we come alive when we hear
the voice of our bridegroom inviting us to come to Him.

—Nancy Guthrie

*W*hy do love stories so move our hearts? J. R. R. Tolkien says that every story that moves the heart does so because it taps into the true story that was planned before the dawn of time and that these stories, though myths, "steer however shakily towards the true harbour."[1]

I love to show the women in prison a scene from the movie *Ever After*. Danielle, the Cinderella character (played by Drew Barrymore), comes to the ball in a shining gown with gossamer wings. She knows she is really just a ragamuffin dressed up, so, caught between fear and hope, she stands at the top of the stairs whispering to herself, "Just breathe."

We are held in suspense until the prince looks up and can hardly believe his eyes. Somehow he knows: this is his true love. His penetrating gaze parts the dance floor, and all in attendance turn to follow his eyes to this mysterious beauty.

Then, as the music swells, he runs, leaping and bounding down the steps, then through the crowd and up the steps to her. Indeed, this is the picture we have in the Song:

Behold, he comes,
leaping over the mountains,
    bounding over the hills.
My beloved is like a gazelle
    or a young stag.
    —Song 2:8–9

This is the gospel, the best love song, the story of the One who did not wait for us to clean up our lives but comes to us first, leaping over the mountains to reach His beloved.

"DEER!"

In the deep woods of Wisconsin where I live, deer are plentiful. In the quiet winter, when the tourists and summer residents are gone, it is not unusual for me to drive down my driveway to startle a half dozen of them, sending them bounding, white tails disappearing into the cedar forest.

But in the summer, they hide. My grandchildren and I often hike, looking for them, failing to find them. How often, I wonder, have we walked right past them, hidden behind the leaves, still as statues? Then when we least expect it, one will bound out, making our hearts stop.

I remember when four-year-old Sadie wanted to be the leader on the stone-lined path that leads through the forest from my cabin to my sister's cabin. She was running in front of me, when suddenly a stag leaped across the path, just yards in front of her. "Deer!" she screamed and ran into my arms, eyes wide with fright.

The Spanish Christian mystic St. John of the Cross commented on how the deer is an apt analogy for our Lord:

It is noteworthy that in the Song of Songs the bride compares the Bride-groom to the stag. . . . She makes this comparison . . . because of the swiftness with which he shows and then hides himself. He usually visits devout souls in order to gladden and liven them, and then leaves in order to try, humble, and teach them.[2]

This is what we see throughout the Song: she loses him and finds him, only to have it happen all over again:

Tell me, you whom my soul loves,
> where you pasture your flock.
> —Song 1:7

Behold, he comes,
leaping over the mountains.
> —Song 2:8

I will seek him whom my soul loves.
> I sought him, but found him not.
> —Song 3:2

Scarcely had I passed them
> when I found him whom my soul loves.
> —Song 3:4

I opened to my beloved,
> but my beloved had turned and gone.
> —Song 5:6

When Christ does not give us what we want, we may feel like He is hiding. But we must ask ourselves: *What is it I really want?* When we turn to God only for what He can give and not to commune with who He is, we are treating Him as our servant and not as our Beloved. But when we desire His presence above all else, we enter into a dance with the Trinity.

Author Larry Crabb urges us to remember that as believers, through the indwelling Holy Spirit, the rhythm is already in us. "The divine fountain could be gushing up out of soul, moving gracefully in rhythm with the song of delight that the Father is singing over me." So if we wonder, *Why am I not dancing?* Crabb suggests the answer:

I'm moving to the wrong tune. The energy flowing out of me is not divine water, it's natural sewage. And it's swaying with the proud, terrified beat of a soul determined to prove itself, to win attention, to gain approval, to feel important, to be seen as powerful, to protect itself, to exercise enough control to make life work for me, whatever that might mean.[3]

It is understandable that we would like our lives to be free of trouble, but God's Word is clear that trials refine us. Trusting Him in the midst of trials instead of just begging for Him to take them away can bring us forth like gold.

Young Christians are often surprised when trouble comes into their lives and God does not immediately deliver them. John Newton, the converted slave trader who wrote "Amazing Grace," observed in his many years as a pastor that the immature Christian thinks that the God who parted the Red Sea for him will always rescue him. Newton observed that young Christians often feel superior because of this dramatic help, thinking they had something to do with their successes, and are therefore judgmental toward other believers who aren't having these same Red Sea partings.[4]

Perhaps that is why God, like a deer, seems to hide sometimes. We wonder, *Where is the God who was so near?* He may be pruning, testing, or waiting to reveal a plan when the time is right. At those times when He hides, it is easy to become discouraged, to feel He must not love us.

When Ron and Debbie put their trust in Christ, they were filled with euphoria and the sense of His presence. But a year later Debbie had a major surgery that was unsuccessful, and she was in great pain for months before doctors realized the surgery had truly failed.

Finally, after many trips to the emergency room, Debbie was readmitted to the hospital to have the surgery redone. She and Ron were understandably anxious about this next surgery. From Debbie's hospital room, Ron texted me, "If this surgery fails, I'm not going to trust God anymore."

I drove down to Green Bay to be with them, to listen, to weep, and to pray. I told them to tell God how afraid, angry, and confused they were. "When you do that, you are lamenting, which is what Psalms, the prayer book of the Bible, shows us to do when God doesn't make sense. He wants you to be truthful with Him—

and then to listen to Him. It is then that He can give you wisdom or peace in the storm."

I left Ron my book *The God of All Comfort,* as well as Mike Mason's book *The Gospel According to Job.* Job's story was meant to comfort suffering believers for ages to come. God hides from Job to test him but also appears to him three times, surprising him, like a deer bounding out, and comforting him with revelations of His love, mercy, and wisdom.

Ron, who has a pliable Play-Doh heart, read both books cover to cover. Then he texted me, "I will trust God even if Deb does not get better."

Tried and found true, Ron was going to trust God, for better or for worse, in sickness and in health. Trusting before God came bounding out, like a deer, healing Deb's body and soul.

What God asks of us when He comes to us—either initially in salvation or day by day in our lives with Him—is to trust Him enough to follow Him, wherever He leads, and to seek Him, even when He seems to be hiding.

RUNAWAY BRIDE

We now come to the climax of new love in the Song, when the bridegroom asks for a full commitment from the peasant woman to come away with him and be his bride.

Many commentators believe that a proposal in the Song happens when the bridegroom runs to the woman, stands outside her lattice, and says,

> Arise, my love, my beautiful one,
>> and come away,
> for behold, the winter is past;
>> the rain is over and gone.
> The flowers appear on the earth,
>> the time of singing has come,
> and the voice of the turtledove
>> is heard in our land.
> The fig tree ripens its figs,
>> and the vines are in blossom;

they give forth fragrance.
Arise, my love, my beautiful one,
　　and come away.
　　—Song 2:10–13

This poetic picture is a return to the Garden of Eden. "'The winter is past,' (verse 13) the long season when love between humanity and God, Israel and God, was cold."[5] Though she has been wise to not hurry love, now the time is right for marriage. He asks her to leave her nest and come away with him.

But she resists! He is all she's ever dreamed of. Finally, her fantasy can become reality. And yet she moves *away* from him, clinging to her own life, heading deeper into her cleft in the rock. Not only must he ask her *twice* to come away, but then he also must *entreat* her with reasons to come out of her hiding place. She seems unreachable to him, and so he entreats.

O my dove, in the clefts of the rock,
　　in the crannies of the cliff,
let me see your face,
　　let me hear your voice,
for your voice is sweet,
　　and your face is lovely.
　　—Song 2:14

Again he calls her "my dove." Doves are defenseless, lacking claws, teeth, and speedy flight. They often tuck themselves away in inaccessible places so that even if they are seen, they cannot be reached.[6] But he is not a predator; he is love itself! Why, oh why, does she resist?

And why do we?

Again, the earthly marriage picture is illuminating.

LEAVING AND CLEAVING

Walter Trobisch was a marriage counselor in Europe, America, and Africa. Trobisch knew that, no matter the differences in cultures, God calls every couple to leave their parents so that they may truly cleave to their spouse and become one flesh. A divided heart cannot cleave, so we must first leave.

Speaking to African couples, Trobisch said that where he lived, in Austria, tears were shed at weddings at the pain caused by this severing between parents and children. Heads nodded. "It is the same here," they said. He writes, "Leaving is the price of happiness. There must be a clean and clear cut. Just as a newborn baby cannot grow up unless the umbilical cord is cut, just so marriage cannot grow up and develop so long as no real cleaving, no clear separation from one's family takes place."[7]

So many marriages suffer because there has been no real leaving. If a man does not put his wife first but defers continually to his mother or if a woman runs home to her parents whenever she argues with her husband, the marriage is in trouble. If a husband cannot stop going out with his buddies every night or if a wife trashes her husband to her friends, they have not left and put their spouse first. They are tearing apart their marriage with their own hands. Parents are to be honored and loved, friends cherished and chosen wisely, but the top earthly priority must be the spouse. A husband and a wife must be closer to each other than to their parents, their friends, and even their children. They must be closer to each other than to their work, their ministry, or anything else. They must leave so that they may truly cleave.

How I remember our first married Christmas. I was so looking forward to going "home," which to me still meant my childhood home with my parents in Wisconsin. Steve and I were planning to take our newborn baby there on December 23. But on December 20, Steve became ill.

Neither Steve nor I knew the Lord at that point, and I was particularly selfish. I honestly was more concerned about getting home for Christmas than I was about Steve's health. As the baby in my family, I had been pampered and entitled. What mattered most to me was me. My parents had always made Christmas magical. I told Steve that it wouldn't be Christmas unless we were in Wisconsin with my parents. Somehow I thought my husband could snap out of whatever he had so that we could be "home" for Christmas.

But instead of getting better that December, Steve got far worse. Though he was always stoical with pain, he was clutching his chest and groaning in agony. I called the doctor, and immediately an ambulance was sent. I followed in our car with our newborn son.

The doctors determined Steve had pericarditis, an infection of the lining of the heart that, at least at that time, was often fatal. When I protested, "He's just twenty-one," they shook their heads. Heart failure could affect anyone—regardless of age. (Steve had smoked two packs of cigarettes a day since his late teens. This was before we knew how dangerous smoking was.)

Two things happened at the hospital that, looking back, I attribute to a merciful God removing blinders from our eyes. Steve was put in a critical-care unit with two other men who were close to death—one was a believer and one was not. The believer was a peaceful young man who was trusting God, praying softly. The unbeliever was cursing God loudly. The young believer died while Steve was in that room. Steve never forgot how real God was to that young man or the radiance he had as he left this world.

Second, when I was told my husband very well might die, I came to my senses. Where we spent Christmas didn't matter anymore. Though I didn't know God yet, I cried out to Him for my husband to live. And in God's great mercy, Steve lived. (He also never smoked another cigarette.)

Both of our hearts were softened toward God that Christmas. (Providentially, my sister would come share the gospel with us the following fall.) And I finally left my parents. I loved and honored them, prayed for them, and spent time with them, but Steve was now my first priority.

Now on the other side as a mother-in-law, I have felt the pain of letting go of my children. I must hold them loosely so that their marriages can grow. This has been a growing process for me, for I was slow to see that my habit of sideways comments was an attempt to control them covertly. It was idolatry, for I was trusting in myself and my ways instead of in God and His ways. But I have repented and am seeing the beautiful fruit of that repentance. Not only do I have sweeter relationships with all my adult children, but also the Spirit my sin had been quenching is now moving visibly in their lives. God is a better Mother and Father than I could ever be.

Leaving can be painful for both sides, but it is necessary for new life to flourish. Only then can two hearts truly cleave together.

The Hebrew sense of the word *cleave*, Trobisch explains, "is to stick to, to paste, to be glued to a person. Husband and wife are glued together like two pieces of paper. If you try to separate two pieces of paper which are glued together, you tear them both."[8]

God intended this cleaving for the security of the marriage and the children. It is why He does not condone polygamy. Likewise, a man and a woman are anatomically designed to fit together, a clear picture of cleaving. God's plan from the beginning was for one man and one woman to leave, cleave, and to become one flesh—and this points to the deeper mystery of the spiritual union between Christ and His bride.

INCLINE YOUR EAR

Jonathan Edwards, the Puritan of such great intellect, saw that Psalm 45 was the Song of Songs in a nutshell.[9] In the Song and in Psalm 45, we hear a love song about a great king who weds a maiden. In each, this king is the fairest of men, his lips anointed with grace, his garments with myrrh. In each, he rides forth with many warriors in splendor and majesty, a sword at his thigh. In each, his palace is described as made of magnificent materials. In each, there is a chorus of companions rejoicing in this wedding day. And in each, he comes to his future bride and asks her to leave her home and come with him. We have already seen that in the Song. Here it is in Psalm 45:

> Hear, O daughter, and consider, and incline your ear:
> forget your people and your father's house,
> and the king will desire your beauty.
> —Psalm 45:10–11

The author of Hebrews in the New Testament quotes Psalm 45 and clearly reveals that the King in that psalm is Jesus (see Hebrews 1:8–9). So what does this mean for us, the betrothed bride of Christ?

When my sister Sally came and presented the gospel to me, it sounded appealing. She told me, though, that although salvation was a free gift, when you came to Jesus it had to be for who He was: Lord of lords and King of kings. He wanted my whole life.

That caused me to pause. I asked her, "If I gave my life to Jesus, would He ask Steve and me to give up the expensive house we are planning to build?"

My sister was quiet for a long time. (She was a new Christian herself and was crying out to God for wisdom.) When she finally looked up, she said, "In your case, I think so—because you've been talking about that house so much that I think it is a god in your life. You think it will fill up the emptiness in your life. The real God is a jealous God and doesn't want any other gods before Him. So in your case, I think the house would have to go. Jesus said, 'Whoever would save his life will lose it, but whoever loses his life for my sake will find it' (Matthew 16:25)."

At that point I was getting wedding jitters as I drew closer to the altar, and I considered becoming a runaway bride. This seemed such a huge commitment to give my whole life to Jesus. But my sister's challenge caused me to try to discover if Jesus really was who He said He was. If His claims proved faulty, I could keep my house. But if indeed He was the God He claimed to be, then I would be a fool to run away. If I became convinced His claims were true, I would leave that house and surrender my plan for my life to Him.

When Sally left, she gave me three books: J. B. Phillips's paraphrase of the New Testament, *Mere Christianity* by C. S. Lewis, and *The Cross and the Switchblade* by David Wilkerson. I read them all because, though I didn't know it, Christ was wooing me.

I'm convinced Sally heard the voice of Jesus when she chose those three books for me. The paraphrase by J. B. Phillips is beautiful and lucid. Because it is just the New Testament, I wasn't tempted to start in Genesis and then get lost somewhere in Leviticus, as so many do.

Mere Christianity appealed to my head with one strong argument after another. I think the primary obstacle for most people in coming to Christ is the fear of losing control, but if you become convinced Christianity is *true,* then a greater and holy fear overtakes you—fear of rejecting the only One who can rescue you from God's just wrath. The clincher for me was this famous argument from Lewis:

> A man who was merely a man and said the sort of things Jesus said would
> not be a great moral teacher. He would either be a lunatic—on the level
> with the man who says he is a poached egg—or else he would be the Devil

of Hell. You must make your choice. Either this man was, and is, the Son of
God, or else a madman or something worse. You can shut him up for a fool,
you can spit at him and kill him as a demon or you can fall at his feet and
call him Lord and God. But let us not come with any patronising nonsense
about his being a great human teacher. He has not left that open to us. He
did not intend to.[10]

And *The Cross and the Switchblade* was for my heart. It tells David Wilkerson's story of seeing God answer prayers so specifically that it left me in wonder,
Could it be that God might be this real, this personal?

A month later, the Spirit of God had so persistently revealed the truth of Christ
to me that I did what I was destined to do before the foundation of the world: I
surrendered to Jesus, leaving as much as I understood at that time and cleaving to
Him. There was much I had yet to learn. God's Word unfolds light gradually—
perhaps if we saw it all at once, it would be too overwhelming. Even with the little
I knew, it felt like a big jump, for it is always hard to leave one's old way of life. But
I had seen enough to know that it was the only thing to do. He was God and therefore He knew best.

I shake my head now when I think that holding on to a house nearly stopped
me from surrendering. How foolish, how young, and how blind I was—for nothing, absolutely nothing, can compare to the beauty of knowing Christ and experiencing His presence and pleasure.

In order for us to become truly one with the Lord, leaving and cleaving must
be something we choose daily. It begins the moment we wake up, before we even
swing our legs out of bed, with our approach to the day. Will it be with hearts of
gratitude and an expectancy to experience God's presence? Will we long to meet
with Him, knowing He wants to see our faces and hear our voices? Will we leave
e-mail, Facebook, the morning news, or any of the calls of this world so that we can
cleave to Him?

Then all through the day we have choices to leave our idols with their siren calls
and continually choose to cleave to Jesus. Nothing is exempt: from what we put in
our mouths to what we put in our hearts, from responding to our surly teen to responding to the slow-as-molasses clerk at Walmart. Will we leave our old sinful
responses that have failed us so many times and instead let Jesus lead the dance?

Many believers never get out of the wilderness because they are not willing to do what it takes to truly cleave to Christ. How do you know if you are fully embracing the radical call to become one with Christ? In *Union with Christ,* pastor Rankin Wilbourne gives two important tests:[11]

> "1. *Are you threatened by it?* . . . Union with Christ gives us a new identity, but to accept it requires leaving behind the life we have always known."

> "2. *Are you comforted by it?* . . . Are you experiencing the freedom and confidence union with Christ brings?"

I personally am amazed at the new freedoms and joys I am experiencing in this third act of my life, and I know it is because I am allowing Christ to replace my heart idols. This is making my wilderness experiences less frequent, since I often now am able to catch those little foxes who ruin my vineyard!

The Little Foxes

In the Song, the Shulammite does not come out of her hiding place in the cleft. She is not yet willing to leave her former life and cleave to the bridegroom. Still, he gives her grace with a gentle warning:

> Catch the foxes for us,
>   the little foxes
> that spoil the vineyards,
>   for our vineyards are in blossom.
>   —Song 2:15

God uses this picture of a conniving fox, sneaking under the leaves to steal the tender new grapes in our vineyard, to show us how destructive seemingly little sins can be. Closing our eyes to the needs of our husbands or closing our ears to the soft prompting of the Spirit can ravage our marital and spiritual vineyards just as little foxes ravage earthly vineyards.

Sometimes foxes come in the form of false teachers. Jeremiah says these false shepherds can destroy God's vineyard, trampling it and turning it into a wilderness (see Jeremiah 12:10).

Recently I got a text from Vicki, who is one of the tender young plants in God's vineyard. A friend had been urging her to read a book by someone I knew to be a false teacher, a man who has led many astray by saying that everything in Scripture is a metaphor, including the Resurrection.

Vicki texted me, asking, "Is it okay to read this book?"

I froze, sensing that the fox was trying to steal the tender new grapes in Vicki's vineyard. I texted back, "No, that author is a false teacher, perverting Christianity. I'm so glad you asked!"

Vicki: "Thanks. I asked because I had a check in my spirit."

Me: "I am amazed that you had a check in your spirit!"

Vicki: "You are amazed? *I* am the one who should be amazed!"

Me: "You are right! ☺ I should know how good He is after all these years!"

God came running to Vicki when the Enemy was lurking. He came bounding for His love when He saw the little foxes in her vineyard. And because she is His sheep now, she recognized His voice and she obeyed.

Of course, it isn't just new Christians who need to watch out for foxes. Every single day we are in a battle between truth and the lies of our enemy. He tells us the same old lie that he has used from the beginning: that God does not really have our best interests at heart and we cannot be happy unless we go our own way. That is a lie from the pit of hell—for the Enemy wants to steal from us the joy and the sense of God's sweet presence that come with obedience.

TAKING GRACE FOR GRANTED

By the close of chapter 2 and the opening of 3 in the Song, it becomes apparent that the Shulammite chooses not to respond to her shepherd-king. Feeling secure in his grace, she chooses not to go with him but rather tells him to go without her and come back to her in the morning, when the shadows flee:

> My beloved is mine, and I am his;
>   he grazes among the lilies.

Until the day breathes
  and the shadows flee,
turn, my beloved, be like a gazelle
  or a young stag on cleft mountains.
  —Song 2:16–17

This reminds me of the many times I have closed my ears to God's prompting, counting on His grace to forgive me and then choosing sin even though I have known it was wrong.

Hudson Taylor, the missionary from the 1800s who founded the China Inland Mission (now OMF International), wrote only one book, and it was on the Song. Here Taylor gives insight into the maiden's thinking:

The bride's response gives a sad illustration of sin's deceitfulness. Instead of bounding forward to meet him, she first comforts her own heart by remembering his faithfulness, and her union with him.

My love is mine, and I am his.
  He browses among the lilies.
  —Song 2:16

My position is one of security; I don't need to worry about it. He is mine, and I am his; and nothing can alter that relationship. I can find him now anytime because he browses among the lilies. While the sun of good fortune shines on me I can safely enjoy myself here without him. If trial and darkness come he won't fail me.[12]

And so she does not leave what feels so safe to her. She tells him to go without her but to hurry back. Look at this again:

Until the day breathes
  and the shadows flee,
turn, my beloved, be like a gazelle
  or a young stag on cleft mountains.
  —Song 2:17

Though this is a challenging passage, light comes when we see that it is used again as the closing of the Song (see Song 8:14). In the close, it is the bridegroom's choice to go, just as Jesus chose to leave us while He went to prepare a place for us. But here, it is her choice, for he has twice requested that she come with him and she is silent. To do nothing is a choice, whether it is to neglect to be with God in His Word or to ignore His prompting to respond to Him.

The Shulammite chooses to endure separation rather than leave her familiar surroundings to be with the bridegroom. Taylor writes,

> Not caring about what he wants, she lightly dismisses him with the thought: "I will enjoy his love later."
>
> The grieved bridegroom leaves!
>
> Poor foolish bride! She will soon find that the things that once satisfied her can satisfy no longer. She will also find that it's easier to turn a deaf ear to his tender call than to find him when he is absent.[13]

The wilderness time has arrived.

LESSON 6: SONG OF SONGS 2:8–17

 Icebreaker

What story, either in a book or a movie, has touched your heart? Can you see how it, as J. R. R. Tolkien suggests, taps into the True love story?

Memory Work

All week, review Song 2:10–13. In the beginning of the study, pair off, say this passage to one another, and share any new insights.

Watch

To understand heart idols, watch my eleven-minute interview on *100 Huntley Street,* titled "Worshiping Idols Without Knowing It."[14]

Read Chapter 6 of *He Calls You Beautiful*

1. What insight did you gain by looking into the Song of Songs?

2. What stood out to you in this chapter or in my video interview and why?

3. Read aloud this week's section, Song 2:8–17. What quickens you from this passage and why?

4. Read Song 2:8–9. Describe the scene. Describe the emotions of the Shulammite.

5. The Shulammite recognizes her lover's voice. How do you recognize God's voice?

6. In Song 2:9, she compares her beloved to a deer. St. John of the Cross writes about the swiftness with which a deer can appear and then hide himself. He says the deer appears "to gladden and liven" devout souls and leaves "to try, humble, and teach them." Share a time when you experienced each of these with God and how those times impacted you.

7. Have you ever had a time when it mystified you that God did not immediately fix a problem, yet later you saw why He did not? If so, share.

8. Read Song 2:10–14. What does the shepherd-king ask the peasant woman to do in verse 10?

   a. What reasons does he give to show her the time is right?

   b. What do you think this means?

   *c. He must ask her again in the second half of verse 13. Why do you think, after so longing for this, that she hesitates?

d. If you are married, did you have any trouble leaving home physically or emotionally? If so, why do you think that was?

e. Doves, being defenseless, hide from predators in the crannies. What does this show you about what is lacking in the bride's understanding of the bridegroom's goodness? When have you been like the bride?

f. In verse 14, how does he attempt to coax her out?

g. Can you hear the voice of Jesus speaking to you in this passage? If so, what do you feel He is trying to convey?

9. From an earthly perspective, what do you think it means to leave home physically, and why is it important to do so?

10. In order to become one with Christ and move out of the wilderness, we must die daily and follow Him. In what areas are you fearful of letting go? In what areas have you experienced great joy and freedom after letting go?

11. Read Song 2:15–17. What warning does the shepherd-king give his beloved?

   a. What could this mean on an earthly level?

   b. What could it mean on a spiritual level?

   c. In verse 16, how does she comfort herself regarding her decision? What would be a spiritual parallel?

d. When does she want him to return to her?

12. Share a time when you were slow to respond to God but later regretted it. How should you handle these regrets?

13. How will you apply this week's lesson to your life?

Prayer Time

If you are willing, pray about your answer to question 13 above and allow the others to support you. For example, if your application is to not let "the little fox" of distraction bother you during your time with God, ask God to help you with that. Another might say, "I agree." And another might say, "If her mind wanders, help her recognize it and get right back on track."

Wilderness Love

Prone to Wander

I Sought the One My Soul Loves

The Pain and Purpose of the Wilderness

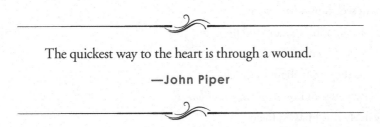

The quickest way to the heart is through a wound.

—John Piper

s a young bride, I blamed Steve for the emptiness in my heart, though it was not his fault. God had set eternity in my heart, but I could not fathom what God had done (see Ecclesiastes 3:11).

Again and again, I unleashed my inner storm of discontent on Steve, sending him out the door for work wounded. I often ruined his day and certainly ruined my own. *We had known such sweetness, but now what had I done? Could he still love a shrew like me?* The hours seemed like days before he would return, and like the Shulammite, I became frantic, knowing I couldn't stand to lose the one my soul loved. I was blessed with a man full of grace who always enveloped me in his arms when I ran to him, stroking my hair, telling me of his love.

That is the emotion we find here in the Song at the beginning of chapter 3. When Christ hides, it is for our benefit, but when we back away from Him, it is because of a lack of trust in Him.

In chapter 2, the bridegroom pleads with the maiden to arise and go with him, but she stays in her cleft. He waits as long as he can and then, for reasons she cannot understand but that are for her good, he suddenly leaves, like a deer bounding off.

She experiences a sleepless night. Finally, in the middle of the night, having come to her senses, she runs out to seek him:

On my bed by night
I sought him *whom my soul loves;*
    I sought him, but found him not.
I will rise now and go about the city,
    in the streets and in the squares;
I will seek him *whom my soul loves.*
    I sought him, but found him not.
The watchmen found me
    as they went about in the city.
"Have you seen him *whom my soul loves?*"
Scarcely had I passed them
    when I found him *whom my soul loves.*
    —Song 3:1–4

As we have seen before in the Song, this repetition of "him whom my soul loves" seems a deliberate echo of the Shema, which tells us to love the Lord with all our hearts, souls, minds, and strength.

Do you see? His absence has brought her to her senses, and she is now seeking the one her soul loves, with all her might. And she does not want his gifts—she wants him!

I relate to this, for it brings to mind the terrible days after we found out that Steve had cancer. Two of our daughters, Sally and Annie, were with me in Indiana, where I was speaking at a retreat. Steve had gone to the doctor because he didn't feel well and wanted to be sure he didn't have an ulcer. Later he called to tell me the news: advanced cancer.

Sally, Annie, and I drove day and night through the rain and through our tears. What we longed for was him! Not what he could do for us but for him.

When we finally got to our home in Nebraska, the three of us rushed in, so eager to hug him, to hold him, to have him be alive. He was lying down on the sofa but sat up with a smile, my ever-cheerful man. Sally and I sat on either side, clinging, wanting to feel his flesh, his warmth, his life. Annie fell at his feet, her arms around his legs, her body heaving with sobs, her silky dark hair spilling onto his lap.

Fourteen months later, we did lose Steve.

Steve and I used to ponder how you could leave and cleave without having your heart eventually broken, for none of us can avoid the parting that death brings. I had written so much about relational idolatry in friendship, and we knew it was important to continually have our marriage be a "threefold cord," where we were helping one another find strength in God instead of in one another. Yet still, when you cleave and one dies, there is a ripping apart. Poet Luci Shaw told me that when her husband, Harold, died, "it was like being cut in half."

But what are we who are left behind to do? When Jesus asked Peter if he was going to turn back, as so many others had done, because the road was hard, Peter said, "Lord, to whom shall we go?" (John 6:68). There is no other safe place to go.

So I sought, with all my heart, the One whom my soul loved. I fell at His feet, clinging to Him as Annie had clung to Steve. I wanted to want only Him. And during that time of the most intense grief, I sought Him "on my bed" during many a sleepless night.

On this earth, we move in and out of the wilderness, from times of taking Him for granted or not trusting Him to times of seeking Him with all our hearts. When the Shulammite does not respond to her bridegroom's call but stays in the cleft of the rock, she moves into the pain of the wilderness. But that pain brings her to her senses and she begins to seek him again.

ON MY BED I SOUGHT HIM

The Shulammite says,

> On my bed by night
> I sought him whom my soul loves;
> > I sought him, but found him not.
> > —Song 3:1

Because an unmarried Israelite woman living in her mother's house would not be looking for her beloved in her bed, this poem speaks to a deeper reality, beyond the physical. It takes us, I believe, to the main point of the Song.

We are to seek the Lord with all our hearts and all our souls and all our minds—*especially* during the dark nights of the soul when Satan wants us to hide from the One we need the most. As Dr. Ellen Davis writes, "In biblical idiom, the bed signifies more than sleep and lovemaking. It is also a place of prayer where God is sought intently, and sometimes in great anxiety, and revelations are granted."[1]

Have you not, like David or Job, sought the Lord in the night on your bed? Often in the night when I wake and anxieties multiply, I begin to pray, seeking Him.

In *The God of All Comfort,* I write about a sleepless night shortly after Steve's death when I sought the Lord, reminding Him that He had promised to be a husband to the widow. I was lamenting, telling Him what was truly in my heart, unleashing my storm on Him:

> O God, I miss Steve so much. In the past when I couldn't sleep, he would
> pray over me or sing over me. You promised to be a husband to the widow!
> But how can someone who is not even flesh and blood ever be that? And I
> do not sense Your presence! O Lord, You have forsaken me, though You said
> You never would.

I curled up in the fetal position and wept. And then, in the midst of drenching my pillow, a memory came to me, taking me back to when I was a first-time mother. The three of us lived in a tiny apartment with paper-thin walls. My job was to keep that baby quiet in the night so our neighbors and Steve (who was both going to medical school and working at a psychiatric hospital to support us) could sleep. So I'd run to our baby at his first cry, unbuttoning my nightgown as I ran so as not to lose time. I'd put him to my breast, but he would not latch on. How he'd wail and flail his little arms and legs! How frustrated I was, for my breasts were engorged with milk, waiting for him. I was coaxing him to find me, and yet he acted like I had abandoned him.

Finally, after several minutes, he would find my nipple, latch on, nurse greedily between gasping sobs, and eventually calm. His little eyelids would go to half-mast and I'd think, *Oh little pumpkin, I was right here all along!*

And then I knew. The Lord was saying the same thing to me: "It's all right, child. I have been right here all along." By lamenting to the Lord, by telling Him the truth, a dialogue had begun. I had sought Him and He responded. This was the beginning of moving me out of the wilderness and into His arms.

HAVE YOU SEEN HIM?

In the Song, the maiden does not find her bridegroom in her bed, so she says, "I will rise now and go about the city" (Song 3:2). Love has made her bold, for she is not afraid to cry out and run about the city square, looking for him, asking the watchmen if they have seen him.

Scarcely has she passed the watchmen when her beloved suddenly appears. She holds him and will not let him go. She takes him back to her mother's house.

Now he knows she is ready to leave her mother's house in order to cleave to him. So though the wilderness has been painful, it has also had a good purpose, showing her what she wants more than anything else. And she wants him! The wilderness may seem cruel, but God allows it so that He might get our attention and show us what we *really* need.

The Song of Songs has powerful parallels to the book of Hosea. Each story has a bride who has trouble leaving. Each story has a faithful bridegroom who does not give up on his bride. Each bride goes through the wilderness. In each story, the bridegroom (Solomon/Hosea) is a dim foreshadowing of the eternal Bridegroom. In each story, the bride (the Shulammite/Gomer) points to His eternal bride. But there are illuminating differences as well.

In the Song, by leaving the maiden to stay in the cleft, the bridegroom simply allows her to experience the natural consequence of refusing to go with him. I believe that, most frequently, the natural consequences of our sins bring us into the wilderness. In His wisdom, God often allows us to reap what we sow, desiring that the wilderness will bring us back to our senses and cause us to seek Him. In the Song, the Shulammite comes to her senses, and her beloved meets her quickly.

But in Hosea, the situation is more severe. The ruts of Gomer's sin are deeper than the Shulammite's, for Gomer has traveled this destructive path many times. She was a promiscuous woman when Hosea married her, and though you might think that marriage to a good man like Hosea would end her promiscuity, it does not. The natural consequences of promiscuity have not brought her to her senses. Her memory is very selective and so she returns to her lovers. She remembers how they gave her good things like oil and drink, while forgetting that they used and abused her. (She is like the Israelites who, though delivered from Egyptian slavery, began to yearn for the garlic and the leeks, forgetting the bondage, the bricks, and the beatings.) In Gomer's forgetfulness she says,

> I will go after my lovers,
>> who give me my bread and my water,
>> my wool and my flax, my oil and my drink.
>> —Hosea 2:5

And Hosea says,

> She did not know
>> that it was I who gave her
>> the grain, the wine, and the oil,
> and who lavished on her silver and gold. . . .
>> [She] went after her lovers
>> and forgot me, declares the LORD.
>> —Hosea 2:8, 13

Gomer cannot stop her self-destructive pattern, so God must actually lead her into the wilderness. It is important to see that this is not punishment (for Jesus took all our punishment at the cross) but discipline designed to help her realize how destructive her false lovers are in contrast to her True Lover.

Look carefully to see the purpose of her time in the wilderness:

> Behold, I will allure her,
>> and bring her into the wilderness,
>> and speak tenderly to her.
> And there I will give her her vineyards
>> and make the Valley of Achor a door of hope.
>> —Hosea 2:14–15

Many of the women I visit in prison are like Gomer in that they have returned to their lovers (such as cocaine or prostitution) over and over again. God has already allowed them to experience the natural consequences of these sins through loss of health or relationships, but they may, like Gomer, persist in their destructive paths. So then, out of mercy, He "leads [them] into the wilderness," making sure they get caught.

Prison is a real wilderness. Every time I go there, I think, *I never want to end up here!* And yet it is so often there, especially when Christians have come in to minister, that the inmates find or return to God. I remember Summer, who sang a beautiful solo in prison before I spoke. She was so young, beautiful, and talented, and I wondered what her story was. She told me afterward:

> I was a Christian, but I drank a lot and was in denial that I was really
> an alcoholic. I had gotten two DWI tickets, but I rationalized each one,
> blaming "overzealous policemen." I prided myself that I could hold my
> liquor, even singing a solo in church after drinking quite a bit. But one
> night after singing in church, I ran a red light coming home and was
> pulled over. It absolutely shocked me in court when the judge sentenced
> me to prison. But here, through the program of Celebrate Recovery, I've
> gotten the help I truly needed. It has been so hard, but I am also so
> thankful.

God's purpose in leading us into the wilderness is always for our good. His purpose is to restore our vineyards that have been trampled by sin, to turn our valleys of pain into doors of hope, to transform our ashes into beauty.

It always saddens us when a woman who truly came to know the Lord in prison falls back into her old ways, embracing drugs or alcohol, once she gets out. I remember going cell to cell with Brady, a faithful young man who volunteers with Linda Strom's organization, Discipleship Unlimited, as I do.

When we came to one cell, Brady said, "Oh no! Amber, I didn't want to see you back here."

"I'm so sorry, Brady." She began to weep.

Brady spoke tenderly to her, not condemning her but endeavoring to give her hope that the true Lover of her soul could break her chains for good.

But it isn't just women addicted to drugs and alcohol who are vulnerable to running back to their old deceitful lovers. We all do it. Hopefully we grow and see a diminishing of our reluctance to leave our old ways of life. As long as we are on this earth, though, we still wander in and out of the wilderness. We will not completely stop running to other lovers, to the Baals (the false gods the Israelites often worshiped), until we see Christ face to face. On that day, this is what Christ will do for us:

> In that day, declares the LORD, you will call me "My Husband," and no longer will you call me "My Baal." For I will remove the names of the Baals from her mouth, and they shall be remembered by name no more.
> —Hosea 2:16–17

How wonderful it will be when I *cannot* sin anymore, when I will not even *think* about running to false lovers but am content to stay under the shadow of my One True Beloved. No longer will my idols tell lies to me, luring me and breaking my heart, for God will take me to His heart and keep me close, as the Shulammite pleads for her bridegroom to do at the close of the Song. He will do what He promised:

> I will betroth you to me forever. I will betroth you to me in righteousness and in justice, in steadfast love and in mercy. I will betroth you to me in faithfulness. And you shall know the LORD.
> —Hosea 2:19–20

Our great wedding will not occur until the day when we see Jesus face to face. But the Song foreshadows that incredible day when we will step out of the wilderness on the arm of our Beloved.

UP FROM THE WILDERNESS

In biblical days, the groom prepared a place for his bride in his father's house and then, when the father said that all was ready, the groom would come for the bride with his companions. A *shofar* horn was blown to signal his appearing. He would take her from her parents' home, and then the bride and groom *together* would travel to the wedding.

Here in the Song, the people see the king bringing his bride up from the wilderness:

> Who is this coming up from the desert
>   like a column of smoke,
> perfumed with myrrh and incense
>   made from all the spices of the merchant?
> Look! It is Solomon's carriage,
>   escorted by sixty warriors,
>   the noblest of Israel,
> all of them wearing the sword,
>   all experienced in battle,
> each with his sword at his side,
>   prepared for the terrors of the night.
> —Song 3:6–8, NIV

How reminiscent this is of God leading His bride, Israel, through the wilderness with columns of smoke. But here the pronoun in "Who is this" is singular and feminine, so we have the portrait of the king bringing a lovely young maiden out of the wilderness.

The bride is wearing myrrh and frankincense. While myrrh was a perfume (see Esther 2:12), frankincense was associated with sacred use—with sacrifices that made "a pleasing aroma to the LORD" (Leviticus 6:15). Her perfume tells us that the bride has been refined in the wilderness, as her ancestors failed to be, and now her surrender is the "living sacrifice" that Romans 12:1 says is so pleasing to the Lord: "When we come before God in true worship, God sees us, not as dutiful, but rather as beautiful, even irresistible, like a bride perfumed for her husband."[2]

The description of the wedding carriage is strikingly similar to the description of Solomon's temple, where man could be intimate with a holy God. Both were made with wood from Lebanon, had posts of silver and an interior of gold and silver, and were inlaid with love. This was the day, we are told, "of the gladness of [the bridegroom's] heart" (Song 3:11). We can only imagine what this day will be like, but we know that Jesus will rejoice over us.

EVERYTHING IS RIGHT

My friend Susan and I were catching up in a booth at our favorite restaurant in Fish Creek when my phone vibrated. I checked the caller ID. "This can wait. It's my son JR—he calls me often with prayer requests. I'll call him after lunch."

Had I answered at that moment, I might have found a flight to Indianapolis and made it to the church on time. For when I called, two hours later, he said, "Mom, you might want to pull over."

Anxiously I pulled into a parking spot. "What's wrong, honey?"

He laughed. "Everything is right! Dianne and I are getting married tonight."

"What? No! Really?"

"Yes, Mom. Really!"

I could hardly believe the news for joy. He and Dianne had faced so many obstacles to getting married, though they had remained pure and faithful throughout a very long engagement. After a lengthy time, and still no set date, I admit that I had begun to lose hope, but they had not! Now they had taken my breath away— and they didn't want to wait a day longer!

"I want details!"

"Because the way finally seems clear, we got our license. This morning we drove down to Brown County to walk, pray, and seek God. Dianne told me that she would love to be married in the little chapel near her home in Indianapolis where she had put her trust in Christ as a child. And she wanted Dr. Riley [her family's longtime pastor and their good friend] to preside. So I called him to see how soon it could happen. But he and the chapel were booked for so far in the future. I felt it slipping away, and my spirit rose up in me and I asked him, 'What about tonight?' Dr. Riley thought for a moment and then laughed. He said they were both free tonight—so Mom, we are getting married at six this evening!"

"And Dianne is okay with so little time to prepare for the wedding?"

"Yes!" At this point he handed Dianne the phone.

Breathlessly happy, she said, "It feels like when Jesus will come back for His bride! In the twinkling of an eye! Please pray I find a dress on our way to the chapel!"

JR got back on: "I *am* sad you won't be able to get here, Mom. Do you want us to postpone?"

"Oh no! Just get married!"

He laughed joyously and told Dianne, "She said, 'Just get married!'"

And so in a whirlwind, they hurried back to Indianapolis, praying Dianne would find the perfect wedding gown on the way. As it turned out, the first dress she tried on was her dream gown and they did make it to the church on time. Two good friends met them there to provide the music and be witnesses.

I've never seen more euphoric newlyweds. On their honeymoon, a waitress asked JR if he knew what his wife would like to drink, for Dianne had stepped away. JR surprised the waitress by throwing back his head and crying, "Yes! She's my wife!"

Marriage is the most intimate and meaningful relationship on earth—and the Lord uses it to communicate what we mean to Him and to show how binding His covenant is with us. The pictures of marriage and of the vineyard in the Song both have the same message: what leads to a joyful life is union and communion with Christ. The vineyard theme occurs occasionally in Scripture, but the wedding theme permeates it. The Bible begins with a wedding, ends with a wedding, and is shot through with pictures and parables of a faithful bridegroom loving and transforming an unfaithful bride.

It is not a coincidence that the first miracle of Jesus—or as John puts it, "the first of his *signs*"—occurred at a wedding (see John 2:1–11). Jesus took those ceremonial water jars representing the ritualistic cleansing and turned them into wine, the joyful sign of the Spirit! The Spirit has the power to do what the Law could never do: the Spirit can make all things new, even an unfaithful bride.

Indeed, one day God will take us completely and permanently out of the wilderness of this world and delight in us as a bridegroom rejoices over His bride. We must not lose heart, as I nearly did concerning my son's marriage. For it is a sure promise that He is coming back to take us as His bride. This is what Isaiah promises:

No longer will they call you Deserted,
    or name your land Desolate. . . .
The LORD will take delight in you,
    and your land will be married.
As a young man marries a maiden,
    so will your sons marry you;
as a bridegroom rejoices over his bride,
    so will your God rejoice over you.
    —Isaiah 62:4–5, NIV

In other words, as the Bible reminds us again and again, one day Jesus will come for us, blow the shofar, and cry, "Yes! She's my wife!"

Lesson 7: Song of Songs 3:1–11

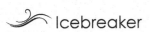 Icebreaker

Have you ever experienced a rift with one whom your soul loves? Describe the pain. Does that give you insight into this passage? If so, how?

Memory Work

All week, review Song 2:10–13.

Listen

In your personal time, prepare your heart for this study by listening to Laura Story's song "Blessings."[3]

Read Chapter 7 of *He Calls You Beautiful*

1. What insight did you gain by looking into the Song of Songs?

2. What stood out to you in this chapter and why?

3. Read Song 3:1–5 aloud. Is there anything here that quickens you? If so, what and why?

4. Read the Shema (see Deuteronomy 6:4–5), which the Jews prayed morning and night. How many times is a phrase from the Shema repeated in Song 3:1–5? Why is this significant?

5. What similarities do you see between Song 3:1 and Psalm 6:6 and Psalm 63:6? Have you experienced a time of seeking the Lord in the night? If so, share.

6. Describe the bride's emotions upon finding her beloved (see Song 3:4–5). Share a time when the Lord came to you when you were desperately seeking Him. Or share your thoughts on my story of seeking God on my bed after my husband died.

The bridegroom discerns that the bride is now ready to leave and cleave. Before you read the wedding scene, get yourself in the mood with the wonderful YouTube video of "Vanessa's Wedding Surprise."[4]

7. Read Song 3:6–11. What quickens you from this passage and why?

8. Describe the scene of Solomon bringing his bride to the wedding. Find all the details you can. What stands out to you and why?

9. How is the picture in Song 3:6 reminiscent of God leading His bride Israel through the wilderness (see Exodus 13:21–22)?

10. Challenge Assignment! Go through Psalm 45 and see how many parallels you can find to the Song. I've started it for you.

   a. Psalm 45:2 and Song <u>6:10 and 6:16</u>

   b. Psalm 45:3–5 and Song <u>3:8</u>

   *c. Psalm 45:7–8 and Song _____

   *d. Psalm 45:8–9 and Song _____

   *e. Psalm 45:10 and Song _____

   *f. Psalm 45:13–14 and Song _____

   *g. Psalm 45:15 and Song _____

   *h. Psalm 45:17 and Song _____

11. In Hosea 2:5–8, why did Gomer return to her lovers?

12. In Hosea 2:14–15, what is God's purpose for Gomer's time in the wilderness? How does this speak to you?

13. What parallels do you see between Hosea and the Song?

14. What is the promise of Isaiah 62:4–5, and what does this mean to you?

15. What is your takeaway and application for this week? Why?

⌒ Prayer Time

In small groups, each woman can share a personal need she has come to understand more deeply through this study. Then take turns supporting each other in prayer.

8

An Oasis in the Wilderness

The Spiritual Meaning of Sex

Profound delight in the other person whose soul seems
to complete mine moves me some distance out of the
self-absorption that seems to be the natural human
condition. This movement of self-transcendence is the
thing that makes sexual love the least inadequate
metaphor and model for the love that we may hope to
feel for God.

—Ellen F. Davis

*A*s long as we live on this earth, we will move in and out of the wilderness.
But God will give us times of great refreshment as He did for David in
Engedi, a delightful oasis in the desert wilderness of Israel, a little Garden of Eden
with a waterfall and flowering fruit trees. It is the secret place where David was refreshed and renewed when running for his life from Saul and his armies.

When the peasant maiden dreams of her wedding night early in the Song, she
says,

My beloved is to me a cluster of henna blossoms
   in the vineyards of Engedi.
   —Song 1:14

Sexual intimacy as God intended it to be is like a beautiful river in the midst of a broken world. It provides a way for a couple to regularly renew their marriage covenant. God designed the marriage bed not just for procreation but also for renewal—just as a river renews, refreshes, and brings life.

This is what the bride is discovering as her groom delights in every part of her during the wedding night in chapter 4 of the Song. She has been dreaming about this becoming a reality from the beginning. It's astounding, but God uses this very earthy picture of consummation to point to that day when we will be presented as a pure bride to Him and He rejoices over us.

A Tent of Protection

What I am so excited for you to see here is twofold: First, you will see how beautiful sexual intimacy can be within God's ordained plan. Second, and much more important, you will see how this good design points to a deeper mystery, a wonder we can only glimpse, when our God will rejoice over us and our land will no longer be called desolate but will be forever like Engedi—forever like Eden!

In the Song, the bridegroom has led his bride up from the wilderness to wed her, to bring her to an oasis. This is the day his heart rejoices over her, and this is the night he delights in every part of her:

> Behold, you are beautiful, my love,
>   behold, you are beautiful!
> Your eyes are doves
>   behind your veil.
> Your hair is like a flock of goats
>   leaping down the slopes of Gilead. . . .
> Your two breasts are like two fawns,
>   twins of a gazelle,
>   that graze among the lilies.
>   —Song 4:1, 5

The groom describes seven of her features, the number of perfection. He uses metaphors of *life* from the Promised Land: her eyes are like gentle doves; her teeth like freshly washed white ewes; her breasts are like the soft heads of twin fawns grazing among the lilies. These metaphors may sound foreign to us, yet the comparisons would delight one living in Israel, for she has seen all of these things. She is a peasant maiden who has seen snowy white ewes, fresh from their baths. She has watched a flock of black goats coming down the mountains of Gilead, their coats gleaming and undulating in the sun.

Solomon has managed to describe his beloved's body in a way that delights her yet protects her modesty. How different this is from the crudeness of pagan love poetry and pornography, which graphically use and abuse women, stripping them of dignity.

Author Mike Mason, in *The Mystery of Marriage,* tells of the wonder of the marriage bed, using images with which contemporary women might more easily identify:

> I still haven't gotten used to seeing my own wife naked. It's almost as
> if her body is shining with a bright light, too bright to look at for very
> long. I cannot take my eyes off her—and yet I must. To gaze too long
> or too curiously is, even with her, a breach of propriety, almost a crime.
> It is not like watching a flower or creeping up to spy on an animal in
> the wild. No, my wife's body is brighter and more fascinating than a
> flower, shier than any animal, and more breathtaking than a thousand
> sunsets.[1]

A woman's body is holy, to be enjoyed in the sacred place of marriage. Leaving (your family or any other loves) and cleaving (covenanting before God and witnesses) is the tent of protection over becoming one flesh (sexual intimacy).

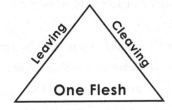

All night long in this sacred space under the tent of leaving and cleaving, the bridegroom delights in his wife, taking in her fragrance and the curves of her

feminine body. Again his delight in her through the night is described with
metaphors:

> Until the day breathes
>   and the shadows flee,
> I will go away to the mountain of myrrh
>   and the hill of frankincense.
>   —Song 4:6

When I was about thirteen, my dad took me on a drive to give me "the talk."
He parked the car overlooking a nearby lake. He was nervous and silent for a long
time. Finally, he looked me directly in the eyes and said soberly, "Dee Dee. A
woman's body is sacred."

I was silent.

"Do you understand?"

I didn't, but I nodded, so wanting this to be over.

Thinking he had accomplished his mission, my dad started the car and we
drove home. I was mystified as to what he was trying to communicate until I was
years older. Today, though my dad is no longer on earth, his words come back to
me and reflect to me the pictures in the Song. The marriage bed, like the Garden
of Eden and the temple, is a sacred, protected space where God smiles upon
intimacy.

Marriage, as the writer of Hebrews says, is holy, and the bed is to be kept
undefiled (see Hebrews 13:4). Purity, both before marriage and within marriage, is part of His design, a riverbank to keep this river pure and life-giving.
Here husband and wife can come away from the wilderness, away "from the dens
of lions, from the mountains of leopards" (Song 4:8), and enjoy an oasis of
renewal.

Do you see the spiritual parallel? Jesus left His Father in heaven and His
mother at the cross in order to cleave and to become, one day, one with His bride.
He asks us to leave other loves and to cleave to Him, anticipating a glory we can
only imagine. On that day, we will find not just an oasis but also a permanent
paradise of love.

MY SISTER, MY BRIDE

It isn't until now, after the wedding, that the shepherd-king calls the Shulammite his bride. He sometimes calls her "my sister, my bride," not meaning that she is his sister but that she is both his lover and his closest friend. (In fact, in Song 8:1 she fleetingly says she wishes he really were her brother, for then she would be allowed to show affection to him in public, something husbands and wives could not do in that culture.) He loves calling her "my bride."

This reminds me of a beautiful young couple in our church. Amy refers to Eric, when she talks to others, as "my husband," and he delights to overhear it, knowing she delights in the fact that he belongs to her. And Eric calls Amy, his ballerina beauty, "my wife" or "my bride," with a smile of pride.

Here in the Song, after the wedding, the bridegroom cannot say "my bride" often enough. Now she is truly his and intimacy is not just allowed but blessed! See how often he repeats this new name for her:

Come with me from Lebanon, *my bride.* . . .

You have captivated my heart, *my sister, my bride.* . . .
How beautiful is your love, *my sister, my bride!* . . .
Your lips drip nectar, *my bride.* . . .
A garden locked is my sister, *my bride.* . . .

I came to my garden, *my sister, my bride.*
　—Song 4:8–12; 5:1

Within the bounds of marriage, sexual intimacy is not just permitted, it's encouraged! Within this tent of protection, there is a joyful abandonment that the unmarried can never know. Despite their words about not needing a piece of paper, in their hearts they do not feel the same protection as those who have promised before God and witnesses to forsake all others and to be true until death—in sickness and in health, for richer or for poorer, and for better or for worse.

Perhaps the change in my life that surprised me (and my husband!) the most after coming to Christ was my increased enjoyment of the marriage bed. In fact, my first published writing as a new Christian was a letter to the editor of *Redbook* about the joy of married sex! At that time, *Redbook* had conducted a sexual survey of a hundred thousand women and could hardly believe their results. This was their cover's headline:

Sexual Pleasure:
The Surprising Results of 100,000 Women

What was shocking? The women who the editors thought would enjoy sex *the least* enjoyed it *the most*. At the top of their charts were strongly religious, married women! I smiled. I pondered. This was even before I was familiar with the beauty of the Song and the deep reality to which it pointed. Even so, God had redeemed our marriage bed with the little scriptural knowledge I had and with the healing His Spirit brings.

I wrote *Redbook,* and they published my letter in the subsequent issue. Men and women stopped me in the grocery store and at the YMCA to comment. I blushed. My sister Bonnie wrote me, "I can't believe my little sister is writing about sex in *Redbook.*"

I didn't intend for my first published work to be on sex, but so it was! This is what I wrote so many years ago:

I am thankful for this survey, for it shatters the notion that strongly religious women don't really enjoy sex. In fact, it shows that the reverse is true. I'd like to offer a few points of explanation for this:

- A woman who has a close relationship with God has experienced healing forgiveness for anything in her past. A woman who hasn't drawn near to God may, without realizing it, be carrying guilt. This is bound to affect adversely her sexual relationship.
- A woman who has a close relationship with God has experienced a peace in Him that's going to affect every aspect of her personal life. A woman who is far from God has an emptiness that cannot be filled with anything but God. She imagines and hopes other things will fulfill her, but they won't.

- A woman who is reading her Bible realizes sex within marriage to be good and pleasurable. Proverbs 5:18–19 tells husbands to "rejoice with the wife of thy youth. . . . Let her breasts satisfy thee at all times; and be thou ravished always with her love" (KJV).

Many Christian women have struggled with abandoning themselves in the marriage bed, and they need to know how God smiles on His good plan. Jill, who did the pilot study on the Song, testifies,

The Song has also completely changed my view of sex. Before, I saw sex as something God tolerated in marriage. But what the world polluted, the Song has sanctified. I sense God's blessing in the marriage bed. A door has opened and released me to be vulnerable and intimately giving.

Our culture today has lost the beauty of sex as God designed it. Though we all need grace for our impure thoughts and behaviors and we must show mercy to those caught in the bonds of disordered love, let us not fall into the deception of thinking it is merciful to let go of God's design for the marriage bed. It is true we will always struggle with temptation in this fallen world, but we must not forget that with God, there is forgiveness, there is healing, and there is always a redemptive plan.

A GARDEN FOUNTAIN

Once when speaking in California, I explained why purity before marriage strengthens a marriage. I said that God has given every newlywed couple who has kept themselves pure a balm of tremendous sexual satisfaction to soothe the hurts they unintentionally inflict on one another as they adjust during that first year of marriage. But if they have dipped into that jar repeatedly before marriage, then they come to that first year of marriage with a jar of depleted balm.

After my talk, a lovely little lady with white hair and a walker came up to me and said, "I liked your point about the bomb!" I hesitated, and then I realized she thought I had said "bomb" instead of "balm." And then she made me laugh as she fairly shouted, "I remember! It was a bomb!"

Whether a balm or a bomb, sex is a gift to those who have kept themselves pure. In the Song, the bridegroom rejoices in his beloved's purity before marriage:

A garden locked is my sister, my bride,
    a spring locked, a fountain sealed.
    —Song 4:12

And on the wedding night, he rejoices when she is unlocked. He compares her to a garden of many delights:

Your shoots are an orchard of pomegranates
    with all choicest fruits,
    henna with nard,
nard and saffron, calamus and cinnamon,
    with all trees of frankincense,
myrrh and aloes,
    with all choice spices—
a garden fountain, a well of living water,
    and flowing streams from Lebanon.
    —Song 4:13–15

In Proverbs, Solomon describes *both* the wife and the husband as flowing waters meant to bring refreshment, renewal, and life. He warns husbands,

Drink water from your own cistern,
    flowing water from your own well.
Should your springs be scattered abroad,
    streams of water in the streets?
Let them be for yourself alone,
    and not for strangers with you.
Let your fountain be blessed,
    and rejoice in the wife of your youth,
    a lovely deer, a graceful doe.

Let her breasts fill you at all times with delight;

> be intoxicated always in her love.

—Proverbs 5:15–19

God wants purity from men as much as purity from women. He knows how an impure man causes destruction. In Hosea, He says He will not hold a double standard (see Hosea 4:14). And in Malachi, He declares He will not hear the prayers of the man who has broken covenant and been faithless with the wife of his youth (see Malachi 2:13–14).

A dear friend of mine who is an author and radio personality was married to a man addicted to pornography. She tells of her heartache when she first discovered his hidden stash of magazines behind the furnace. The addiction continued and she found herself withdrawing emotionally. During marital intimacy, she felt their bed was filled with the women of his fantasy world: airbrushed, voluptuous vixens. My friend is a particularly passionate beauty, but her husband's ongoing addiction quenched her flame. Sex became a duty and a burden to her. Though she tried to abandon herself, she could not. She tried with all her might to make the marriage work, but it eventually ended in divorce.

My friend went on to raise her son as a single mother. Years later, when her son was nearly grown, she married a godly, sensitive pastor. A few months after the wedding, she and I lunched together at a little Asian restaurant in Chicago. There, over pad thai and tiny cups of steaming ginger tea, I asked, "What have you been thinking a lot about lately?"

"Sex," she said immediately. Then she blushed to the roots of her red hair.

I laughed, both at her honesty and for the joy of belonging to a God of second chances.

With tears in her eyes, she said, "I never knew how wonderful and beautiful sex could be when each of you knows without a doubt that you are the only one for the other."

There is a beauty in the God-ordained boundaries for sex: one man and one woman for life. When you know you are the only one, when you trust your spouse, you can abandon yourself in a way you simply cannot in the face of infidelity.

I made a plate with "Proverbs 5:18–19" printed on it to remind Steve to rejoice in me and me alone. He carried it in good humor to church potlucks. When asked what that reference was, he smiled, explained that I had given the plate to him, and said they should look up the verses in private.

Do you see the spiritual parallels here? Within marriage is a garden of delights for us, but we must not eat of fruit outside that garden. Similarly, in the Garden of Eden, God told Adam and Eve that they could eat of any tree in the garden except one. Satan always wants us to crave the forbidden, knowing it will rob us of intimacy with one another and with God.

The Song is filled with pictures meant to ring bells in our souls of the new Eden, the Promised Land. We see the four rivers of Eden watering its lush gardens and representing the joy God has planned for His bride: a restored Eden, a permanent place of refreshment and delight. Not only is the bride a garden of delights, she is like a "land flowing with milk and honey" (Deuteronomy 11:9):

> Your lips drip nectar, my bride;
>> honey and milk are under your tongue.
> —Song 4:11

In fact, the whole Song moves us out of the wilderness and toward Eden. Eden is not only the setting but also "the object of love, especially as the perfumed mountains and lush fields of Israel are at times identified with the lovely 'topography' of the woman's body."[2]

How deep, how rich, how multilayered is this Song of Songs.

AWAKE, NORTH WIND!

The bride, feeling secure in her husband's love, says,

> Awake, north wind,
>> and come, south wind!
> Blow on my garden,
>> that its fragrance may spread abroad.
> Let my lover come into his garden
>> and taste its choice fruits.
> —Song 4:16, NIV

While the south wind is a warm, gentle wind, representing sweet things in life, the north wind is a cold, harsh wind, representing the trials of life. But now, after being refined in the wilderness, the bride is open to both winds, giving thanks for them and trusting that God is in control. With this attitude, the fragrance of her Lord will spread everywhere!

Recently I taught on this truth at a retreat. When I sat down afterward at my table, the young emcee told me he had been taught this passage from a very literal perspective—and he had never been able to understand the north and south wind or why the fragrance would spread everywhere. To me it was an affirmation of what we have lost by seeing the Song so exclusively from an earthly, sexual perspective. We *can* learn things that enrich our earthly marriages, but that is not the central point. Marriage is lovely, but it is not the best. It points to a much deeper mystery: the love story between God and His beloved.

And so the honeymoon of Solomon and his bride is, as honeymoons are meant to be, euphoric. But it doesn't take long for the honeymoon to end and the bride to lose her passion. We're not out of the wilderness for good yet!

Lesson 8: Song of Songs 4:1–16

 Icebreaker

Has your view of the marriage bed changed because of the Song? If so, how? Do you think non-Christians would be surprised by the Bible's view of sex? If so, why?

Memory Work

This week, learn Song of Songs 2:14–17. Memorize it all at once, and then review, review, review, adding it to Song of Songs 2:10–13.

Read Chapter 8 of *He Calls You Beautiful*

1. What insight did you gain into God's plan for the marriage bed and the spiritual reality it foreshadows?

2. Read Song 4:1–8. Is there anything here that quickens you? If so, what and why?

3. In Song of Songs 1:14, the bride compares her beloved to "a cluster of henna blossoms in the vineyards of Engedi." What was Engedi? What could this teach you about one of God's purposes for the marriage bed?

*4. Throughout the Song are images of the beautiful land of Israel, and some-
times of Eden, which are compared to the loveliness of the Shulammite's
body. Find some of them in the groom's description of her in Song 4:1–7.

5. In its descriptions of sexual intimacy, how is the Song different from pornography and racy romance novels?

6. If you are married, how might you praise your husband's body, character, and
passion in poetic ways? You may or may not want to share this in the group,
but be sure to share it with your spouse!

7. Read Song of Songs 4:8–16 aloud. Does anything quicken you? If so, what
and why?

8. For the first time, the shepherd-king calls the Shulammite woman his bride. How many times does he call her this? What is the significance of this?

9. Ephesians 5:31–32 draws a parallel between the leaving, cleaving, and becoming one flesh of marriage and the relationship of Christ and His bride. Let's reflect on this parallel as it is reflected in Song 4.

  a. The king sees the Shulammite woman as beautiful, brimming with life, and without flaw. What does it mean to you that Christ sees you the same way, as His beloved? How could this help you today (see also Isaiah 62:5)?

  b. He praises her for being a "garden locked" (Song 4:12) before the wedding night. What are some ways you can remain pure and faithful while waiting for your ultimate Bridegroom? (One way is explained in 2 Corinthians 11:21.)

  c. The bride's passion for him and him alone is like a garden of fragrances unsealed. What might be the spiritual application of this?

10. When teaching the next generation about sexual intimacy, the talk is full of "Thou shalt nots." Using the Song or Proverbs 5:18–19, write what you might say to a youth about the beauty of the marriage bed.

11. Read Song of Songs 4:16 again. What might the north wind represent on a spiritual level? What is the north wind in your life right now? How could you respond to the north wind so that God's fragrance might spread abroad?

12. What might the south wind represent on a spiritual level? What is the south wind in your life right now? How could you respond to the south wind so that God's fragrance might spread abroad?

13. What is your takeaway or application from this week's study?

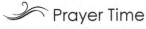 ## Prayer Time

In clusters, each woman can share a personal need that she has come to understand more deeply through this study. Then take turns supporting each other in prayer.

The Lukewarm Bride

When the Honeymoon Is Over

Just as your desire for intimacy with your spouse is a reliable indicator of your marital health, so too your desire for intimacy with Christ is a reliable indicator of your spiritual health.

—Douglas Sean O'Donnell

$\mathcal{R}$ ecently our women's Bible study group had a great laugh when Debbie, who has been married to Ron for fifty years, tried to text him while he was out of town but accidentally sent the message to our whole Bible study instead of to Ron. Each of us got this surprising text on our phones: "I am counting the days until you are home. How I miss you in our bed!"

We teased them that their marriage must be in good shape. Debbie blushed and Ron grinned.

When, after decades of marriage, the sexual intimacy is still vibrant, it means the marriage covenant is being continually renewed. Scripture encourages us not to shut out a spouse sexually (see 1 Corinthians 7:5). Not only can this leave a couple wide open to temptation, but they are also failing to avail themselves of the renewing grace of the marriage bed. For just as communion can renew one's covenant with the Lord, communion in the marriage bed can renew a couple's covenant with each other. It is the time to heal any breach and to say, once again, "I truly love you. I don't want anything between us."

A friend of mine tells of being on a family vacation with her son and his wife.

"After listening to them fight all day long, I thought, *Is this marriage going to make it?* Then the next morning they were so lovey-dovey I thought, *Who are these people? They weren't here yesterday!* But then I realized, *They got a fresh start.*" They rolled to the middle, reached for one another in repentance, and responded in cherishing each other physically. God designed the marriage bed not only for procreation but also for renewing the marriage covenant.

In Song of Songs 5, we see what happens when passion fades and is not intentionally renewed. This earthly picture of a lethargic bride points to the spiritual condition that theologians have called torpor, or spiritual sluggishness. Here in the Song, the honeymoon is over and the desire that had been at a rolling boil is now as tepid as tea left overnight on the nightstand.

When Our Beloved Knocks

This passage opens with the image of a bridegroom who is tender, patiently knocking, persistently waiting, calling his beloved again, "My sister, my love, my dove, my perfect one." He has been waiting so long that his head is wet with dew:

> I slept, but my heart was awake.
> A sound! My beloved is knocking.
> "Open to me, my sister, my love,
>   my dove, my perfect one,
> for my head is wet with dew,
>   my locks with the drops of the night."
> —Song 5:2

What does it mean when the Shulammite says, "I slept, but my heart was awake"? Some think she is dreaming, but others, and I agree, believe this passage describes spiritual sluggishness, as when the disciples fell asleep in Gethsemane. Jesus's friends let Him down at His time of greatest need. I'm sure when they looked back at that moment, they were overwhelmed with regret.

I can so identify. I was in such denial when my husband was dying, somehow believing he was definitely *not* going to die, that I continued to keep many of my speaking engagements. I feel I let Steve down in his time of greatest need.

Jesus gave the disciples grace, and I know He (and Steve) gives me grace as well. But I want to learn from my failure; I want to be able to hear and respond to the Spirit's still small voice and fling the door wide open when He knocks. For so often if we delay, it is too late.

In the Song, the bride *does* delay, offering the weakest of excuses:

I had put off my garment;
　how could I put it on?
I had bathed my feet;
　how could I soil them?
—Song 5:3

What is she choosing over her beloved? Comfort, convenience—herself! I think every married woman has been there. She loves her husband, but she is exhausted at the end of the day and just wants to go to sleep. In my marriage, I found that if I could die to my initial feelings of weariness, my husband was able to get me in the mood, for the Lord made me, as a woman, to be a responder. I had to choose that initial small death, giving my husband the chance to initiate, so that the instincts God created in me could respond. Then I was always so glad I did—for his sake, for mine, and for the sake of our marriage.

On a spiritual level, this is equivalent to shutting out the Lover of our souls because we *think* we know better how to meet our needs. But we are being deceived, because running to our idols by overworking, overeating, or overindulging in anything under the sun only brings us pain and shuts out our shy Lover, robbing us of His presence and power.

Just as God made women responders, the souls of both men and women are responders, for the soul is always feminine in Scripture. When Jesus whispers to our souls, it may take a little death to obey, but then He will take us the rest of the way.

How do we overcome our resistance to dying that little death?

Gazing at Each Other

Philosopher Dallas Willard, in his book *Hearing God,* uses the parable of the talents to explain why we may be slow to respond to God. The man who buried his talent told the Lord, "Master, I knew you to be a hard man . . . so I was afraid, and I went and hid your talent in the ground. Here, you have what is yours" (Matthew 25:24–25). This is why we bury our gifts, or stay in the cleft, or delay in opening the door. We are afraid. We do not in our heart of hearts believe God is good, loving, and altogether for us.

This is why I pray that we as Jesus's bride will return to the Song of Songs, not as a marriage manual, but as a book of love to us. He is the One who says,

> Arise, my love, my beautiful one,
>   and come away.
> O my dove, in the clefts of the rock,
>   in the crannies of the cliff,
> let me see your face,
>   let me hear your voice,
> for your voice is sweet,
>   and your face is lovely.
>   —Song 2:13–14

God invites us to look to Him and enjoy Him looking at us. If we spend enough time gazing on God's beauty, our souls are more likely to respond, to die that little death, and go with Him. And here is the exciting part: Each time we choose the light over the darkness, each time we choose love over hatred, He takes us further into His light and His love and it becomes easier to respond to Him the next time He knocks. He takes our mustard seed of faith and makes it grow.

I know this is true, for I have experienced it in overcoming the heart idols that threaten to deceive me. For example, I have a heart idol of comfort, running to food when I am stressed or depressed. Though this has been a weakness for me all of my life, it nearly destroyed me after Steve died. Instead of running to Jesus, I walked, in a somnambulant state, to the pantry, trying to find solace in chips, chocolate, or even Fig Newtons, which I dislike. (I buy them for guests because usually they do not tempt me.)

In two years I gained twenty pounds, my self-hatred grew, my health deteriorated, and I was not sensing the presence of God as I once had. Yet Jesus did not stop knocking. My pain, from grief and from the overeating that increased my grief, helped me to finally turn to the only One who could help me. On my iPhone I began to listen to sermons, particularly ones by Tim Keller.[1] That was my tiny response, my opening the door a crack. And God came to me, taking me the rest of the way. I sensed His presence, and then I wanted more.

Soon I was listening to several sermons a day, often while I rode my bike through Peninsula State Park, a forest lining Lake Michigan on this thumb of Wisconsin. As I sailed through my Father's world and listened to my Father's Word, I began to find comfort that the false lovers in my pantry were never able to offer.

I also became familiar with Ezekiel's teaching on idols of the heart (see Ezekiel 14:3). God opened my eyes that idolatry is always the sin beneath the sin. Overeating was my visible sin, but the sin beneath that sin was idolizing comfort through food, running to it instead of to God. When I responded to Jesus, choosing to run to Him by listening to sermons, His light began to penetrate the darkness of my heart idol. That light grew as I walked in it, and though it will be a lifelong battle, at least for now that particular heart idol is subdued. I have lost the twenty pounds, my health is being restored, and I have the joy of seeing fruit in my vineyard. But best of all, I am sensing God's presence, like a flowing river of life, in a way I have never experienced before. Are there little foxes in my vineyard? I think there will always be on this earth. But I am much quicker to catch those varmints before they steal my joy!

KNOCKING, KNOCKING, KNOCKING

If I shut my ears to God's still small voice, my world darkens and my heart cools toward Him. That is where we find the bride now in the Song. She has so cooled toward her groom that she cannot be bothered to put on her robe or rewash her feet. She leaves him standing outside, waiting, and knocking, knocking, knocking. Finally he leaves, but first he does something so like our Lord.

The keyholes in biblical days were huge, for you could put your hand through them. The bottom had a ledge, and before he departs, he leaves a gift of myrrh on that ledge (see Song 5:4–5). He was showing her that he still loved her and was giving her grace, just as Jesus gave the sleeping disciples grace when He said, tenderly, "The spirit indeed is willing, but the flesh is weak" (Matthew 26:41). We let

Him down, we quench His Spirit, but if we are His, we can never put His Spirit out.

In the book of Revelation, we have an almost identical picture to this one in the Song. Jesus comes and knocks at the door of His lukewarm bride in the church of Laodicea. To all the other six churches in Revelation, Jesus gives both a commendation and a rebuke. But to the church of Laodicea, there is only a rebuke:

> I know your works: you are neither cold nor hot. Would that you were either
> cold or hot! So, because you are lukewarm, and neither hot nor cold, I will
> spit you out of my mouth.
> —Revelation 3:15–16

Then He entreats them:

> Behold, I stand at the door and knock. If anyone hears my voice and opens
> the door, I will come in to him and eat with him, and he with me.
> —Revelation 3:20

Though this passage is often used to present the gospel, it is actually a picture, as in the Song, of God coming to His bride, who is no longer eager and responsive to His call.

In the book *War Room,* Elizabeth is a real-estate agent who is irritated by the persistent spiritual questions from her client Miss Clara.

Miss Clara asks, "So if I asked you what your prayer life was like, would you say that it was hot or cold?"

Elizabeth says it is somewhere in between, thinking that will be the end of the discussion. Then Miss Clara serves Elizabeth a lukewarm cup of coffee. Elizabeth sips it, grimaces, and asks, "Miss Clara, do you like your coffee to be room temperature?"

"No, baby, mine's hot."

Elizabeth gets the point.[2]

Moderation is good in most things, but not when it comes to loving Jesus. In fact, it is as distasteful as the water in Laodicea. Though Laodicea was an extremely wealthy city, they had bad water. They had to pump their water from cool springs through miles and miles of pipe in the hot desert. By the time it got to Laodicea, it was lukewarm. It was also filled with distasteful minerals. So this metaphor resonated with them!

What had happened to the church at Laodicea that caused their passion to cool to such a disgusting state? Jesus declares,

> You say, I am rich, I have prospered, and I need nothing, not realizing that
> you are wretched, pitiable, poor, blind, and naked.
>   —Revelation 3:17

Author Joseph Stowell in *Jesus Nation* explains that Laodicea was wealthy because it was on a major trade route. It was a banking center, a medical center, and a seller of coveted textiles and eye salve. When an earthquake devastated the region in AD 17, Laodicea was the only city that told Rome that they needed nothing.

But Jesus tells them otherwise. He says,

> I counsel you to buy from me gold refined by fire, so that you may be
> rich, and white garments so that you may clothe yourself and the shame
> of your nakedness may not be seen, and salve to anoint your eyes, so that
> you may see.
>   —Revelation 3:18

Laodicea had plenty of gold, linens, and salve—but now God instructs them to buy gold, garments, and salve from Him. What does He mean?

"Gold refined by fire" refers to faith that is genuine. Peter wrote to the early Christians who were being persecuted, telling them to rejoice in their trials,

> so that the tested genuineness of your faith—more precious than gold that
> perishes though it is tested by fire—may be found to result in praise and
> glory and honor at the revelation of Jesus Christ.
>   —1 Peter 1:7

How do we get genuine faith? We ask Him for it. Then we respond each time He knocks and our faith grows.

What are the white linen garments? The righteousness Christ imputes to us when we put our trust in what He did at the cross. We keep our garments clean by humbly recognizing our propensity toward sin and being faithful to repent when we sin. Those who continually repent as soon as they get out of the light find that God is faithful and just to cleanse them from all unrighteousness.

And what is the eye salve? It is the anointing from the Spirit for which we must continually ask so we can see things as God does.

Laodicea's wealth was a problem for her spiritually—she did not realize she was actually "poor, blind, and naked." We see that wealth has put the Shulammite in the same dangerous position.

THE DANGER OF A TROUBLE-FREE LIFE

It is no coincidence that the most vibrant churches of the world are in the less wealthy countries, in prisons, and among the poor. We can so easily trust in ourselves when life is easy.

The Shulammite no longer has to work under the hot sun in her mother's vineyard. She is the bride of the wealthiest king in history. She has servants, a palace, and the best of food and clothing. She has become lethargic toward the bridegroom, who once enthralled her.

Finally, after her groom has waited for her all night, her heart begins to pound for him (see Song 5:4). She goes to open the door. When she puts her hand to the lock, she finds he is gone but that he has left a gift of liquid myrrh on the keyhole.

> I arose to open to my beloved,
>> and my hands dripped with myrrh,
> my fingers with liquid myrrh,
>> on the handles of the bolt.
> I opened to my beloved,
>> but my beloved had turned and gone.
> My soul failed me when he spoke.
> I sought him, but found him not;
>> I called him, but he gave no answer.
>> —Song 5:5–6

Finally, she awakens to what she needs the most. She runs out into the night in her nightgown, seeking the one her soul loves, and the watchmen misjudge her, indeed, persecute her:

> The watchmen found me
>> as they went about in the city;
> they beat me, they bruised me,
>> they took away my veil,
>> those watchmen of the walls.
> —Song 5:7

THE WATCHMAN BEAT ME

Who are these watchmen? Some see them as true shepherds disciplining the sheep. But the severity of their discipline leads most to believe that they were false shepherds, false watchmen who persecute believers from within the church community. "In rabbinic traditions slapping a person and pulling off his mantle are considered among the most serious acts of insult."[3]

It is not uncommon for a passionate believer to be misunderstood, even by her family or those within the community of believers. Michal, who was David's wife, hated David when he danced before the Lord. Eli, who was a priest, assumed Hannah was drunk when she was praying with passion. How frequently it happens that when someone puts her trust in Christ, she finds to her surprise that she is warned by her minister. He himself may not truly know the Lord and so he is alarmed by her passion. Or he may be so territorial about his own church that he is concerned another church community has awakened her spiritually.

Remember also that the bride represents not just individual believers but the corporate bride of Christ. The Enemy has often come against the corporate bride through those who pretend to be part of the church but are wolves in sheep's clothing. Author and radio host Eric Metaxas writes concerning Hitler,

> In public he often made comments that made him sound pro-church
> or pro-Christian, but there can be no question that he said these things

cynically, for political gain. In private, he possessed an unblemished record
of statements against Christianity and Christians.[4]

And as he gained popularity, Hitler formed a new "evangelical German
church," the "National Reich Church" that portrayed the Aryan race as superior.
Hitler declared Jesus "our greatest Aryan hero" and portrayed him as hating Jews.
Hitler took the rebukes Jesus made to the Pharisees as evidence that He opposed the
Jews. Many Germans who claimed to be Christians joined that church, either because they were deceived or afraid. The pastors of these churches, though called to
be watchmen, were actually tools of Satan, who comes to lie, kill, and destroy.

Now, in the Song, just when she is seeking the bridegroom with her whole
heart, she is beaten and bruised by the watchmen. But their persecution only makes
her try harder to find him. When she found the myrrh on the ledge, it stirred
memories, memories that make her seek him with all her heart. Her faith is tested
by the beatings of the watchmen, but it is genuine, for she will not give up. She has
repented, her garment cleansed again, and she has been given salve for her eyes, for
she sees clearly now. She knows what she really needs, so she turns to the daughters
of Jerusalem and pleads,

> I adjure you, O daughters of Jerusalem,
>> if you find my beloved,
> that you tell him
>> I am sick with love.
> —Song 5:8

Persistence in the face of persecution is a powerful testimony. The daughters of
Jerusalem watch this bride in wonder and cannot help but ask,

> What is your beloved more than another beloved,
>> O most beautiful among women?
> What is your beloved more than another beloved,
>> that you thus adjure us?
> —Song 5:9

When we trust the Lord amidst suffering and persecution, our trials and our trust blaze a trail that leads others to Christ.

The world was shocked when Islamic militants posted videos of the beheadings of twenty-one Christians on a Libyan beach in February 2015. The grisly video showed tall men in black hoods towering over men in orange jumpsuits kneeling on the beach. Twenty of those men were young Coptic Christians from Egypt, but one man, Mathew Ayairga of Ghana, somehow got corralled in with them. Each Christian was asked to deny Christ. When a man refused, he was beheaded or shot. Finally they came to Mathew and asked him, "Do you reject Christ?"

He said, "Their God is my God." And he died with his brothers. Their passion for Christ gave Mathew the same passion.[5]

We may not face martyrdom, but we have an enemy who wants to beat us with lies, shame, and fear. His goal is to get us to back up from the One we need the most.

What is the antidote to all this? Worship. As the bride begins to tell the daughters of Jerusalem why her beloved is better than others, she finds herself moving permanently out of the wilderness and into the land of invincible love.

LESSON 9: SONG OF SONGS 5:1–9

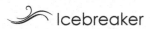Icebreaker

What are some ways the Lord knocks on your door? What are some ways you have responded positively? Negatively?

Memory Work

Review Song of Songs 2:10–17. In the beginning of your study time, pair off and repeat this passage to one another.

Read Chapter 9 of *He Calls You Beautiful*

1. What did you learn about the earthly picture of marriage and how it relates to the spiritual relationship between Christ and His bride?

2. What stood out to you in this chapter and why?

3. Read Song 5:1. What does this tell you about God's view of the marriage bed?

4. Read Song 5:2 and describe the bridegroom's entreaty to his bride. What is a clue that he has been knocking for a while?

5. Contrast her response to her husband in 5:1 with her response in 5:3.

6. Many describe the state the bride is in as torpor, or spiritual sluggishness. What do you think causes this? What incorrect beliefs might we be embracing if we feel this way in our relationship with God?

7. If you are married, have you ever had to die a little death to respond to your husband sexually? What spiritual parallel can you see?

8. What things do you tend to run to when you are sad or stressed? Why do you think you run to your heart idols instead of to the Lord? What is the result?

To prepare your heart for the parallel passage in Revelation 3, watch the three-minute YouTube video from Joseph Stowell titled "The 7 Churches of Revelation—Laodicea's history."[6] (If you like it, he has two more short videos on Laodicea.)

9. What did you learn about Laodicea's history? What contributed to the lukewarm state of believers there?

10. Read Revelation 3:14–22. Did anything quicken you as you first read this?

a. What similarities do you see to Song 5?

b. How did the Laodiceans see themselves in verse 17? How did Jesus see them?

c. Laodicea had plenty of gold, linens, and eye salve. But now Jesus tells them they should buy these things from Him! On a spiritual level, what does each of these items represent and what does each mean to you?

11. Read Song of Songs 5:4–6 and then describe what stirs the bride's heart and awakens desire.

12. Read Song 5:7–9. Describe the severe reaction of the watchmen to the bride. Who do you think these watchmen were and why?

13. Persecution has often come from within the church from false shepherds. Give an example from history or your own life.

14. How does the bride respond to this persecution, and what reaction does it prompt from those watching? What does this teach you about how you need to respond to persecution?

15. What is your takeaway or application from this week's study?

 Prayer Time

In clusters, each woman can share a need she has that she has come to understand more deeply through this study. Then take turns supporting each other in prayer.

Invincible Love

It Is Well with My Soul

The Fairest of Ten Thousand

How Worship Brings Us Out of the Wilderness

We worshiped our way into this mess, and by God's grace,
we will worship our way out.

—James Noriega

I met lovely Nam through the friendship of our daughters. Seven-year-old
May and her mother, Nam, had flown from Thailand to our little Mid-
western town where Nam married Jerry, a businessman who had met her in Thailand. When I invited Nam for tea, her homesickness was palpable. She kept saying
she was glad I was her friend. I thought, *Okay, I better really be her friend!* My
friend Shell joined in befriending Nam as well.

Nam and Jerry opened a restaurant, and Nam was working hard when Jerry
had first one stroke and then another, which left him partially paralyzed and handi-
capped. Nam was pregnant, and bills began to mount. Nam came to Shell and me
to present Jerry's "American" ideas for making money. "How about we have a party
where we sell your church friends soap or lipstick?" she asked.

I squirmed. Shell shot me an uncomfortable glance. I felt the same discomfort
at entering into the world of sales parties. I was glad I could truthfully say, "Nam,
you'd likely lose money getting into one of those networking groups."[1]

Nam quickly shifted to plan B: "How about an American garage sale? Jerry has
a lot of stuff we don't need."

Shell said, "Good idea, Nam, but we should wait until spring. That's when people start looking in the paper for garage sales."

"But we can't wait!" Nam implored Shell and me with her deep brown eyes.

How could we say no? We enlisted a few more friends and threw ourselves into hosting a winter garage sale.

On Monday we put an ad in the paper for the following Saturday, hauled in card tables and bags and boxes of Jerry's and our excess stuff, set up heaters in Nam's garage, and got to work marking things. By Thursday, snow was predicted for Saturday, so we huddled together and prayed while Nam watched us:

"Oh Lord, please hold back the snow!"

"Lord, if it pleases you, please help people see that ad and want to come!"

"Please provide for Nam and Jerry."

"We ask all this in Jesus's name."

When we looked up, Nam was wide-eyed with wonder. "Will your God hear you?"

Nam's god, represented by a clay Buddha, sat in her foyer with offerings of fresh orange slices. We felt like Elijah with the prophets of Baal at Mount Carmel. With mustard seed faith, we said, "Yes!" And silently we prayed, *Please, God!*

In God's mercy, that Saturday was like a day in spring. Scores of people were eagerly buying. Nam made more than enough to pay their bills. She smiled and said, "Your God heard you!"

This was the beginning of showing Nam what it was like to belong to a *living* God who heard, who cared, who provided, and who laid down His life for us.

Why is our God the true God, the most beautiful and gracious and alive God? We see echoes of this question in the Song, as the bride's friends ask her about her groom and she responds with starry-eyed excitement.

A VERBAL STATUE

Remember how in the fifth chapter of the Song, the daughters of Jerusalem ask the bride,

What is your beloved more than another beloved,
O most beautiful among women?

What is your beloved more than another beloved,

> that you thus adjure us?

—Song 5:9

Although the daughters of Jerusalem have been singing praises to this shepherd-king, here it appears that they may not understand that He is the *only* one deserving of such worship. On a spiritual level, this may mean that they represent those who see many gods as praiseworthy. So the way the bride explains why her beloved is better than others becomes particularly fascinating.

It is as if she is describing a statue with a head of finest gold, arms like rods of gold, and legs like alabaster columns on bases of gold. At first this seems odd, for the pagan gods were represented by statues, but Israel was forbidden to create any "graven image" of their *living* God (Exodus 20:4, KJV).

Dr. Ellen Davis believes that this is "a daring move on the poet's part," since a "*verbal* statue" would be as close as the poet could come to representing God with such physicality without transgressing that command.[2] Although this verbal statue has similarities with the statues that Israel's pagan neighbors erected of their gods, there are critical differences.

First, *this* statue is brimming with life—life reminiscent of the flowers, fragrance, and flowing streams of the Garden of Eden.

His eyes are like doves

> beside streams of water,

bathed in milk,

> sitting beside a full pool.

His cheeks are like beds of spices,

> mounds of sweet-smelling herbs.

His lips are lilies,

> dripping liquid myrrh.

—Song 5:12–13

This statue *lives*! And this statue is *relational*—his eyes are focused on her. When he speaks, he is gentle and soothing. This is a *living and caring* God.

This statue also has similarities to the idol that frightened Nebuchadnezzar in a dream, but again with crucial differences. Nebuchadnezzar's statue, though it had a head of gold, had a body made of increasingly inferior metals, ending in feet made of iron and clay. Daniel interpreted the head as representing Nebuchadnezzar's kingdom but the chest, thighs, and legs as inferior kingdoms, each supplanting the kingdom before it. The feet represented a divided kingdom that would not hold together. Bible commentator Matthew Henry writes that these inferior metals were "all of one and the same spirit and genius, and all more or less against the church."[3] Whoever these kingdoms represent, they are *all* eventually broken by the stone cut "by no human hand" (Daniel 2:45) leading to "a kingdom that shall never be destroyed" (Daniel 2:44). This pagan statue not only was vulnerable, but "its appearance was frightening" (Daniel 2:31). This god wanted to *hurt* you! In contrast, the verbal statue of the Song is "altogether desirable" (Song 5:16).

We may think we don't worship idols today, but we do—idols that hurt us. Counselor David Powlison says, "Whenever there is a destructive strand to my thinking and emotions and actions and words, there is something under that we could call an idol."[4] We *worship* ourselves, the approval of others, and the pleasures of this world, thinking they have power to make our lives better. Instead, these idols make a mess of our lives. Idols pretend to be our friends, but like Nebuchadnezzar's idol, they crumble, forsaking us and leaving us with a pile of ashes.

I have received so many e-mails in response to my book *Idol Lies,* which explores the idea of idols in more depth. Kristi, for example, wrote that when she was studying *Idol Lies,* she was in the painful position of realizing that her company was unethical—the company at which she thought she had landed her dream job as a speech pathologist. Members of her church encouraged her to resign. She felt, before God, she needed to do that:

> As I sat in the meeting with my boss, he said cruel things about me, attacking me personally. Before I'd read *Idol Lies,* these words would have been devastating. But I was face-to-face with my biggest fear and able to lean into God's love. Worshiping God instead of my boss and career was liberating. The meeting that should have devastated me smashed the idol of human approval that had been on the throne of my heart for far too long.
>
> God miraculously provided a new job. It is only thirty hours per week, and a new idol began to replace the idol of wanting others to accept me. I

began to question my worth because my workweek was shorter than that of so many others who seemed important in their busyness. But I realized that instead of finding my identity in a life of a busy career, I had to find my identity in Christ alone. It has been such a sweet season of rest in Him.

Our heart idols are terrible, like the statue of Nebuchadnezzar, but Jesus is altogether lovely, like the verbal statue of the Shulammite.

I AM MY BELOVED'S

When the bride tells the daughters of Jerusalem why her beloved is better than others, it does something in her heart.

C. S. Lewis writes of how he once struggled with the idea of praising God: "We all despise the man who demands continued assurance of his own virtue, intelligence, or delightfulness."[5] But does God have any actual need of our praise? Lewis realized praise and worship might be for *us,* for what it does in *our* hearts.

> The most obvious fact about praise . . . strangely escaped me. I thought of it in terms of compliment, approval, or the giving of honour. . . . I had not noticed how the humblest, and at the same time most balanced and capacious minds, praised most, while the cranks, misfits and malcontents praised least.[6]

Being intentionally grateful changes us. The Westminster Catechism tells us that man's "chief end is to glorify God and enjoy him forever." The truth is, by glorifying Him, by praising Him, we *do* enjoy Him.

Let me tell you about Joseph, another friend from pickleball games at the YMCA, who absolutely radiates the joy of Christ. In his eighties, Joseph is probably our oldest player, so he doesn't sprint like some of our younger players on the court. One day I listened in horror as a man balked at having Joseph as a partner, saying, "Do I have a choice?" I wanted to clobber him, but Joseph just smiled and served the first ball (excellently). I thought, *Joseph's confidence in God's love buffers man's unkindness.*

Joseph and his wife adopted all five of their children and have faced many trials, including repeated jail sentences for one of their children. When someone commiserated with him, he said, "God gave us exactly the children we needed and who needed us."

What is Joseph's secret for his seemingly irrepressible joy and graciousness?

In part, he credits his journal of thanksgiving. Over coffee with Joseph and his wife, I asked him how keeping that journal had impacted him. He told me,

> I call it Joseph's Little Book of Blessings. I write in it first thing after the coffee is ready. My wife is still sleeping and our little condo is quiet. I sit down with the journal and make a list of all the blessings of the previous day, and sometimes I include some anti-blessings also. I don't want to call them curses, because they, too, flow from God's love for me. They are just the disappointments that flow from my own desires being in imperfect alignment with God's will for me. I mark the blessings with a filled-in circle and the anti-blessings with an open circle. There are many more filled-in circles than open circles. I found that by concentrating each morning on the good things that happen to me, I find myself happier than before I practiced this—grateful for God's benevolence and power. In wonder I ask, *Why me?* I am not an exceptional man or an unusual Christian—whatever seems otherwise was put there by God. I just reflect His love.

It is not wrong to reflect on the good fruit you see in your life, for, just as Joseph said, it "was put there by God." Being grateful to God for the fruit in your life is a form of praise, for you know that fruit is an organic work of the Spirit of God, not of your efforts. Jesus said, "As the branch cannot bear fruit by itself, unless it abides in the vine, neither can you, unless you abide in me" (John 15:4).

At the close of the Song, the bride asks her bridegroom to go into the vineyards, for she is excited to see new fruit:

> Come, my beloved . . .
> let us go out early to the vineyards
>> and see whether the vines have budded.
>> —Song 7:11–12

When we see ourselves changing, we know it is the Spirit living in us. That is so exciting and helps us persist in going deeper with Him.

Something else then happens in us that is critical. We become less focused on ourselves and more focused on Christ, more habitually praising Him, and more habitually leaning on Him. We see this now happening to the bride, for when she finishes praising her beloved, she makes a statement that is similar to one she made much earlier, but with a crucial difference. Earlier she said,

My beloved is mine, and I am his.
—Song 2:16

But now she reverses the order:

I am my beloved's and my beloved is mine.
—Song 6:3

Do you see? When we first come to Christ, we are still so self-centered, exalting in the fact that Christ is ours and in the many ways He blesses us. In our infancy, we are still often using Him instead of worshiping Him. But as we mature, moving toward the land of Invincible Love, we, like John the Baptist, decrease so that He might increase (see John 3:30).

As a young speaker, I often told the listeners the amazing things the Lord had done for *me*. Today, I want their hearts to melt with the beauty of *Christ*. Our incessant desire to promote ourselves and our own needs is replaced by a desire to glorify Christ and make Him known. We become eager to follow the exhortation of Romans 12:1: "Present your bodies as a living sacrifice, holy and acceptable to God, which is your spiritual worship." Worship is more than praise, more than gratitude; it is the attitude of our whole lives being focused on serving and glorifying God instead of serving and glorifying ourselves. And when the corporate body is doing this, we become as awesome as an army with banners, marching forth against the spiritual forces of darkness.

Citing extensive and groundbreaking research, *Christianity Today* reported the enormous impact throughout history of protestant Christian missionaries—an army with banners we see around the world today. "Why did some countries become democratic, while others went the route of theocracy or dictatorship? . . . Devastatingly thorough analysis [shows] that conversionary Protestants are crucial to what makes a country democratic."

This research also revealed that Christians founded nearly every orphanage and hospital in the world. The abolition of slavery has been due primarily to the tireless prayer and courageous effort of Christians. It is Christians who have risked their lives throughout history to minister to those with cholera, the bubonic plague, AIDS, and Ebola. It is Christians who have led the fight against child labor, the sex trade, and abortion. It is Christians who have fought against apartheid and racism. It is Christians who hid the Jews in Nazi Germany. It is Christians who are bringing light and redemption to the lives of prisoners throughout the world. There is so much that is beautiful about the body of Christ.[7]

THE SECRET OF RADIANCE

As we seek to worship God with all we have, we reflect more and more of His beauty, just as the moon reflects the sun. I have dedicated this book to my dear friend and partner in prison ministry Linda Strom. (Linda founded Discipleship Unlimited.) The secret for her radiance is that she is deeply in love with Jesus. When she visits me at my cabin, she delights in spending the morning with Him, and when she comes out of her prayer closet (a bedroom overlooking the lake), her face shines like I imagine the face of Moses did after he had been with the Lord.

Despite the fact that she is in her early seventies, Linda still flies to Africa to encourage prison ministry there, and she still scoots on her bottom from cell to cell on the cement floor to listen to women pour out their hearts to her. Her radiance has drawn thousands into prison ministry. They have become as awesome as an army with banners, reducing the recidivism (rate of return) in the prisons where she has established "faith dorms"[8] by almost 65 percent! No wonder the bridegroom praises her:

> Who is this who looks down like the dawn,
>> beautiful as the moon, bright as the sun,
>> awesome as an army with banners?
> —Song 6:10

So much more could be done if glorifying God was our highest goal, for then the sad divisions in the body of Christ would also cease. The closing chapters of the Song, which we will look at next, put us in the now and the not yet. They are akin to Martin Luther King Jr.'s "I Have a Dream" speech. King dreamed of a day when the races would live together in love and peace. The poet of the Song dreams of a time when all divisions that now mar our beauty as the corporate bride are gone. He dreams of a time when we will be dancing together in perfect harmony, entering into the dance of the Trinity, dancing right into the war zone, confident that the Lord is our shield and very great reward.

LESSON 10: SONG OF SONGS 5:8–6:10

Icebreaker

If you were to ask people on the street how Jesus was different from the gods of other religions, what answers might you hear? What would you say?

Memory Work

Review Song of Songs 2:10–17.

Read Chapter 10 of *He Calls You Beautiful*

1. What stands out to you in this chapter?

2. Read Song of Songs 5:8–9. What did the bride plead for from the daughters of Jerusalem, and how did that arouse their curiosity?

3. Read Song of Songs 5:10–13 and describe the signs of life in this verbal statue.

*4. Contrast the verbal statue of Song of Songs 5:10–16 with the statue of Nebuchadnezzar's dream in Daniel 2:31–35. What are some key differences?

5. Although we may not worship statues of stone or wood, we do have idols of the heart (see Ezekiel 14:3). Instead of allowing God to be our approval, we crave human approval. Instead of running to our Father's arms, we run to His gifts (like material things, food, even friends) to be our comfort gods. Instead of surrendering control to our loving God, we hold on to the reins of our life, wanting to be our own god. What idols do you see at work in your life? Why is Jesus a better Savior than any of those idols?

In your private time, meditate on Jimmy Needham's song "Clear the Stage."[9]

6. In Song 5:16, how does the Shulammite woman describe the bridegroom's mouth? What bells of allusion does this ring?

7. Have you been kissed by the King recently through His Word, His presence, or His tender mercies? If so, how?

8. We praise God because He commands it, but it is for our good that He does. Based on Scripture and your own experience, how does praise help you? (If you need help, see Psalm 22:3 and Acts 16:25–34.)

9. How could you develop a better habit of praise?

10. Worship is much more than praise. Meditate on Romans 12:1: "I appeal to you therefore, brothers, by the mercies of God, to present your bodies as a living sacrifice, holy and acceptable to God, which is your spiritual worship." With this verse in mind, consider what a life of worship would look like on an ordinary day.

11. Compare Song of Songs 2:16 and 6:3. What difference do you see, and why is this important?

12. Read Song of Songs 6:4–10. Does anything quicken you from this passage? If so, what?

13. The groom compares his bride to Jerusalem (see Revelation 21:1–4). How could God's bride also be a city?

14. His admiration for her is expressed in terms of *life* in the land of promise. How do you see this in Song 6:4–7?

15. Give an example of the corporate bride being "awesome as an army with banners." Have you ever been privileged to minister with such an army? If so, describe what that was like.

    In your private time, listen to "You Are the Sun" by Sara Groves.[10]

16. How does the shepherd-king describe his bride in Song 6:10? What does this remind you of?

17. What is your application from this lesson and why?

᪾ Prayer Time

In small groups, begin with praise for the One who is better than others. Then share your application from this chapter and turn it into prayer. For example, if your application is to praise the Lord more, you could pray, "Please bring to my remembrance my desire to praise You more, and help me better integrate this into my life."

The Dancing Shulammite

Bringing Peace and Good News

The Spirit is calling us to dance with him into the war zone, fully armed and prepared to destroy the enemy with grace, with spiritual power.

—Larry Crabb

*M*y friend Twila was a vibrant mother of five; then in her forties she went into a severe clinical depression that lasted ten years. She tried everything under the sun to be delivered—confessing and repenting of any known sin, counseling, eating right, exercising, various antidepressants, alternative medicines—all, it seemed, for naught. She was rollerblading ten miles a day, but whenever she got to the five-mile mark to turn around, she would plead, *Please, Lord, just let me die.*

Twila says that though she knew all the right doctrines about God, though she had endeavored to serve Him with her whole life, His love had not truly dropped from her head to her heart. And indeed, I am convinced that the central purpose of the Song is to move God's love from our heads to our hearts, to help our *souls experience* God's love.

During those ten years, Twila's counselor kept stressing the love of God to her. She had Twila constantly in the Word and reading books about God's love for her, such as *Abba's Child* by Brennan Manning. Twila chose to allow God to show her His love so that her soul would *respond* to Him.

It wasn't a quick fix. But slowly, as Twila contemplated God's love in His Word, His love moved from her head to her heart. Today, Twila is one of the most joyful women I know. She memorizes whole books of the Bible (Hebrews, James, Romans, Ephesians, 2 Corinthians). When I asked her why she so loved to memorize, tears came to her eyes and she said, "Because when I do, I experience His presence."

Mysteriously, because Jesus *is* the Word, His presence inhabits His Word. And "in [His] presence there is fullness of joy" (Psalm 16:11).

Sometimes Twila travels with me to speaking engagements where she has an opportunity to tell of how God delivered her from depression. She has memorized Psalm 18 to do so. "David had a literal army chasing him," Twila explains, "but my enemy was depression. And truly, 'the cords of death entangled me,' but 'I cried to my God for help' (Psalm 18:4, 6, NIV). He heard my cry, and this is what He did:"

> The earth trembled and quaked,
> > and the foundations of the mountains shook;
> > they trembled because he was angry. . . .
> He reached down from on high and took hold of me;
> > he drew me out of deep waters.
> He rescued me from my powerful enemy,
> > from my foes, who were too strong for me. . . .
> He brought me out into a spacious place;
> > he rescued me because he delighted in me.
> —Psalm 18:7, 16–17, 19, NIV

Twila and some other dear friends came on a cruise where I was speaking. Twila walked round and round the whole ship on the deck where the lifeboats hung and it was empty of sunbathers. She'd review her memorized books of the Bible and use them as a springboard for prayer. At night she'd go back, skipping around as she exulted in the sea, the stars, and the sense of God's presence. This woman who once struggled to put one foot in front of the other was skipping like a little girl.

Twila is a picture of the transformation we see in the bride who, in the closing verse of chapter 6, is dancing boldly between two armies! How different she is from the woman who once asked the shepherd-king not to look at her! And, significantly, for the first time, this dancing bride is called "Shulammite" (Song 6:13).

THE SHULAMMITE DANCING
BETWEEN TWO ARMIES

This word *Shulammite* is never explained in the Bible, nor is there a city named Shulam. The root letters of Shulammite are *sh-l-m,* which would "immediately connote to a Hebrew speaker the notion of *shalom,* 'peace, well-being.' "[1] She is also the counterpart to Solomon (Hebrew *Shlomo*—again from the same root). Therefore, the bride and the shepherd-king are "Mr. and Mrs. Peace."

Also, throughout the Song, we have seen a link between the woman and the holy city, between her body and the land of Israel. She is the bride of Christ, yet she is the "new Jerusalem." She is loved, just as Jerusalem is "the joy of all the earth" (Psalm 48:2). The Hebrew word for Jerusalem, *Yerushalayim,* is also rooted in *shalom* and means "foundation of peace." So, as Mike Reeves explains, she is Mrs. Solomon, or Mrs. Peace—but she is also Jerusalem.[2]

David chose as his capital Jerusalem, which is situated in the southern kingdom of Judah and not far from the northern kingdom of Israel. It was Solomon's unfaithfulness, his disobedience in marrying foreign wives, that ultimately caused this sad divide.[3] At times, Judah and Israel were two armies warring with each other. God's people were neither at peace with God nor with one another.

In the same way, today the body of Christ is often not at peace with one another. We have sad divisions between Bible-believing denominations and even within our own local churches. It is our heart idols, our passions at war within us, that cause quarrels and fights (see James 4:1). Will God's people ever be completely at peace with God and with one another? Yes! John shows us that one day a "new Jerusalem . . . prepared as a bride adorned for her husband" will come down from heaven and God will dwell with us and we shall be his people (see Revelation 21:2–3).

The call "Return, return, O Shulammite" (Song 6:13) would have resonated with the original hearers of God's call to Israel to return to Him:

> Return, O virgin Israel. . . .
> How long will you waver,
>   O faithless daughter?
>   —Jeremiah 31:21–22

Likewise, on an individual level, the psalmist calls,

Return, O my soul, to your rest;
   for the LORD has dealt bountifully with you.
—Psalm 116:7

When our souls are at rest with God, we also become at rest with one another. Decades ago, as I was writing, ironically, *The Friendships of Women,* a bitter quarrel sprang up between me and my closest friends! The setting? A mothers' prayer group. The quarrel? The *right* way to raise children. We argued over dating age, schooling choices, movies, and so on. One by one, my friends left in tears, until only my closest friend, Shell, remained. I then proceeded to tell her that I thought she was being too strict as a mother! Then Shell left in tears. Devastated, I went to Steve and asked, "How can I write a book on the friendships of women? All of my friends have just left in tears."

Wisely, he told me, "When there is a problem in a horizontal relationship, there is almost always a problem in our vertical relationship with God." His words caused me to seek God and then to repent: first to Him, then to Shell, and then to the other women.

Romans 14 tells us not to judge one another on these peripheral issues but to be firmly persuaded in our own minds for our own choices. God restored peace among us, and we continued to pray for our daughters together. The Enemy had wanted to cause a permanent division, but our God brought peace, as only He can. In the next few years, we saw our daughters bond, pray, and be used of God to bring many of their high school friends to Christ.

Do you remember when David prayed, after his great sin of adultery and murder, for God to create in him a clean heart? That psalm goes on to say,

Restore to me the joy of your salvation,
   and uphold me with a willing spirit.

Then I will teach transgressors your ways,
   and sinners will return to you.
—Psalm 51:12–13

Being at peace with God and one another fills us with joy, with dancing! And like the Shulammite, we can have the kind of dancing feet that bring the good news to others!

HOW BEAUTIFUL ARE THE FEET

In chapter 7, the bridegroom begins praising her again, from the tips of her toes to the top of her head. He begins with her feet, the beautiful dancing feet that carry her to tell others the good news of His love.

> How beautiful are your feet in sandals,
>> O noble daughter!
>> —Song 7:1

This verse reminds us of Isaiah:

> How beautiful upon the mountains
>> are the feet of him who brings good news,
> who publishes peace, who brings good news of happiness,
>> who publishes salvation,
>> who says to Zion, "Your God reigns."
>> —Isaiah 52:7

This is what I have seen in my friend Twila. The peace and joy she has found with God is a magnet that draws others to her. Then she has an open door to dance into their lives and bring the good news of the Savior.

Two years ago I joined Twila, her pastor husband, and another couple to plant a church here in northern Door County, the thumb of Wisconsin, which juts into Lake Michigan. Less than 15 percent of northern Door County residents even name a church they consider theirs (and they might attend only on Christmas Eve and Easter). Over half of our churches do not teach the atonement or the physical resurrection of Christ. Though Door County is famous for its bountiful cherry orchards, her spiritual orchards are sadly lacking. So our church is named the Orchard. We have a dream of a spiritual orchard bursting with fruit; we seek to reach those who may have experienced religion but have never experienced the redemptive love of Jesus.

Careful research reveals that church plants are the most effective means of evangelism—for its members are so encouraged to reach out. I am certainly experiencing that thrill as we have been planting the Orchard, not wanting to take from other churches but from the vast fields, white unto harvest, of unbelievers. Though many of the residents of Door County are older, we know and continue to see that it is not too late for Christ to transform their lives.

The YMCA is one of our primary mission fields. As I have shared, Twila and I play pickleball there. A man named Lyle was particularly kind to us when we first started. Soon Twila discovered that she and Lyle shared a passion for gardening. So when hornworms began plaguing Twila's garden, one day on the sidelines she asked Lyle if he knew how to kill them.

"Kill them?" Lyle said with astonishment. "Twila, aren't you a Christian?"

Twila laughed. "Yes, I am! But those hornworms are devouring my tomatoes!"

"You shouldn't kill them; you should capture them."

She laughed again. "And *then* what do I do with them, Lyle?"

"Bring them to me. I'll find a home for them."

And so Twila brought a huge jar of ugly hornworms to Lyle, and a fun friendship began. Yet right away Lyle made one thing very clear: "Twila—you must promise not to try to change me."

Twila promised.

But as Twila and Lyle began to talk of deeper things, sometimes what the Lord was doing in Twila's heart simply overflowed into her words. She would stop midsentence and apologize, remembering her promise.

"No! No!" Lyle protested. "This is who you are. I don't want to stifle who you are. Finish what you were saying!"

It wasn't long before Lyle encouraged his wife, Vicki, to attend our women's Bible study. Lyle didn't really know what he was getting Vicki into—he told her I was a motivational speaker and he thought she could use a little motivation, for she had told him she no longer felt her life had a purpose.

We were doing my investigative Bible study *Examining the Claims of Christ* using the gospel of John. It is a seeker study, which is especially designed for unbelievers: short, simple, and centered on getting to know the real Jesus. I have found that many people who are resistant to church are still interested in Jesus and in what the Bible says. Often they are surprised that Jesus is quite different from what they imagined. Preacher Charles Spurgeon has compared the Bible to a lion in a cage: you don't have to defend it—just open the cage and let Him out!

One day as we were noting the constant tension Jesus had with the religious leaders, I said, "How Jesus hates religion!"

Vicki sat straight up and wrote something in her notebook. She later told me that was a turning point for her. Those who were religious but lacked love had hurt her. But Jesus drew her to Him more and more. She felt she had always believed in God, but Jesus hadn't been that important. She learned through John's gospel that in rejecting Jesus, she was rejecting God. *Oh,* she thought, *I'd better do something about that.*

One day Vicki was curled up in her favorite spot: their porch swing, which looks out on Lyle's gorgeous garden. She was reading Tim Keller's *The Reason for God.* As she sat there, a sense of God's love overwhelmed her:

> I realized that Jesus paid for my sin in full. I felt like He was washing layers
> of dirt from me and bringing me back to the faith I had as a little child, but
> higher up and deeper in. There, looking out at the beauty of His world, I
> knew I was His, and I gave myself a hug.

Our church decided to do Alpha, the powerful evangelistic curriculum, as an outreach. Vicki planned to come and prayed Lyle would too. She suggested to Twila that she invite Lyle. But when Twila invited him, he was hesitant. Understandably, he wondered if he would feel like a target. But to Lyle's credit, he thought, *I have been drawn to what I see in Twila and other Christians, so I would be foolish not to investigate.* So Lyle came, and he came faithfully and enthusiastically.

Near the end of the series was a session on evangelism. Often non-Christians detest the whole idea of evangelism. I thought, *Oh no—this might turn Lyle off.* But in our small group, he said, "That was the best lesson ever!" I thought, *Oh Lord—I think Lyle has become a Christian!*

The next day, while sitting on the pickleball sidelines with Lyle, I so wanted to know if this dear man was now His. I finally said, "Lyle, I have a question for you."

But immediately a man called to Lyle from the court to be his partner and Lyle jumped up from the sidelines to play.

I thought maybe he didn't hear me or maybe God just wanted me to wait for Lyle to tell me if and when it happened. But as I was leaving the gym, Lyle called out to me. "Dee!"

"Yes?"

"Come here!"

Obediently I walked over to him, nervous, for now some of the pickleball players taking down the nets for the day were listening in. We had an audience.

"You had a question for me."

"Oh, Lyle, I decided not to ask it."

"No. You had a question. Ask it."

I hesitated. Lyle is an expert in pickleball, and I think he was expecting a pickleball question. Lyle stepped nearer and cocked his head. Quietly, I asked, "Lyle, have you put your trust in Christ?"

He hadn't expected *that* question! "Not yet!" Then, sternly, "*Why* do you ask?" (He probably thought I was looking for a scalp for my belt!)

"Because, because . . ." And then what flowed out surprised us both: "Because I love you."

"Oh!" He blushed! Then he stammered, "Well, I love you too."

We had one more Alpha meeting after that. I learned later that as Vicki and Lyle were driving home after that meeting, Vicki said, "Lyle, what did you think of Alpha?"

"Before I went, I didn't believe in God and now I do."

Vicki tells this with tears. "He is seventy-six, but God has won his heart." Recently Lyle was baptized in the lake in front of my home.

God has gifted Lyle with an ability to draw others out and find ways to serve them. And now Lyle is using these God-given gifts for God's glory. He is not ashamed of the gospel, for he knows firsthand the difference it can make in a life.

That is the power of the gospel. And blessed be the feet that bring it—the dancing feet! When filled with the love and the joy of the Lord, we are like the dancing Shulammite, joyful Pied Pipers. Together we dance into the vineyards that God causes to bear fruit.

In the Song, as the shepherd-king continues to praise his bride, his phrasing and imagery bring to mind pictures of fruitfulness, fertility, and blessing. "Your navel is a cup of the moon," like the full moon. Her belly is a heap of wheat. Her breasts are like clusters of grapes. Dr. Ellen Davis pictures a harvest moon shining on a fertile land—the dry ground of Israel has become a lush land of abundant crops and vineyards.[4]

LET US GO EARLY TO THE VINEYARDS

Twice in this closing section of the Song, the bride goes down to the vineyards to "see whether the vines have budded" (Song 7:12; see also Song 6:11). The first time she goes alone, wondering "whether a few blossoms had survived the chilly winter of her frosty coldness toward her husband." Not only have they survived, but she is also "caught up into the clouds in raptures" with her kinsman prince.[5] It reminds me of Paul being caught up into the third heaven (see 2 Corinthians 12:1–2). Although experiences of this kind of ecstasy may be rare among believers, it is possible for every believer to experience His enveloping love and peace.

As my friend Twila has become convinced of God's delight in her, her vineyard is bearing much fruit. One change I have enjoyed watching in Twila is her increased confidence. For example, she used to think that being a loving wife meant silently going along with everything her husband suggested, even when she disagreed. Not only did suppressing her thoughts have a negative impact on her emotions, she also began to see that she was being an unhelpful helpmate, caving in to her approval idol and failing to trust God to show her when to share. Now when she disagrees with someone, if she feels led, she has the courage to speak the truth in love. Her husband has received this change positively and others have too, for she is such a gentle messenger.

Twila is also finding the confidence to do dramatizations of her memorized passages. During a particularly acrimonious political season in America, she presented Habakkuk, along with video visuals and commentary. Afterward, a new Christian named Lara said, "I didn't even know there was a book called Habakkuk, but now I will remember this night for the rest of my life."

As chapter 7 in the Song closes, the bride boldly asks her husband to go with her into the vineyards, knowing that what he finds will delight him. No longer is she ashamed of her vineyard. She is eager to show him how pregnant it is with buds, blossoms, and pomegranates in bloom:

> Come, my beloved . . .
> Let us go out early to the vineyards
>   and see whether the vines have budded,
> whether the grape blossoms have opened
>   and the pomegranates are in bloom.
> —Song 7:11–12

There, she will give him her love (see Song 7:12–8:4), again, showing the mysterious parallel between marital intimacy and the intimacy that is better than any bliss we have known on earth. This is an intimacy we cannot even comprehend now, but it awaits us one day, the day when we no longer see through a glass darkly but will know as fully as we are known (see 1 Corinthians 13:12). What a dance we will have then!

LESSON 11: SONG OF SONGS 6:11–7:13

 Icebreaker

The Shulammite is dancing, experiencing the peace of God. Share a time, if possible, when God brought peace to your troubled soul or peace between you and another.

Memory Work

Review Song of Songs 2:10–17 in pairs, sharing any new insights.

Read Chapter 11 of *He Calls You Beautiful*

1. What two things stood out to you the most in the chapter?

Watch the short video testimony from Twila regarding Psalm 18.[6]

2. What comments do you have on Twila's testimony?

Prepare your heart with the song "How Beautiful" by Twila Paris.[7]

3. How has the body of Christ (in this study if you are doing it in a group, or elsewhere if not) been a blessing to you? Be specific!

4. Read aloud Song 6:11–7:13 and share anything that quickens you and why.

*5. In Song 6:11–13, the Shulammite woman goes down to the orchard alone to see if it has survived the frosty winter of her coldness to her husband. Then something amazing happens (see verse 12). What happens, and what could this mean?

*6. In 6:13, she is asked to return. Compare this to Psalm 116:7. What parallels do you see? What are some ways you can return to the rest of the Lord throughout the day?

*7. In 6:13, the bride is called Shulammite for the first time. The root letters *sh-l-m* would immediately connote to the Hebrew reader *shalom*, or peace. Knowing that, why might the name *Shulammite* not be fitting until now?

8. Solomon's name has the same root letters of the Hebrew word for "peace," and likewise, Jerusalem in the Hebrew has the root letters of *peace*. Both the literal Jerusalem and the body of Christ have often not been at peace. Yet what is John's vision in Revelation 21:1–2? What do you think this means for our future?

9. Have you experienced dancing with your sisters in Christ as you advance against the evil forces of this world that seek to divide and destroy? If so, explain.

10. Compare Song 7:1 with Isaiah 52:7. How can feet be beautiful?

11. What feet brought the good news to you? Have you had the privilege of bringing the good news to someone and seeing a transformation? If so, share briefly.

12. Read Romans 10:11–18. What promise do you see in verses 11–13?

    a. What four rhetorical questions are in verses 14–15? What is implied?

    b. What insight does this context give you about beautiful feet?

    c. How does verse 18 reason that everyone everywhere should be aware of God?

    d. People are aware (though they may suppress the truth) of a Creator, yet beautiful feet are needed to bring the message of the gospel. Be still before the Lord and ask how you could better share the gospel as an individual and with your sisters. Share what He impresses on your heart.

13. Read the bridegroom's praise of the dancing Shulammite in Song 7:1–9. Find as many pictures of fertility and abundance as you can. Compare this to Isaiah 41:18–20. What do you see?

14. The woman's body and the Promised Land seem almost interchangeable in the Song. She represents the land we will one day know when we live with the Prince of Peace. What does this mean to you?

15. How might you apply this week's lesson to your life?

 Prayer Time

Fill this in: "Lord, help me dance like the Shulammite instead of worrying about _____ because Your banner over me is love." If you are in a group, support one another with prayers of encouragement. When there is a pause, the next woman should pray her sentence.

The Best Is Yet to Come

The Song's Final Crescendo

If I feel physically as if the top of my head were taken off,
I know *that* is poetry.

—Emily Dickinson

---

ommy opened a door . . ." That is all that is needed, G. K. Chesterton says, to fire a three-year-old's imagination.[1] We are fascinated by a good story, and God is the best storyteller. He tells a love story that seems too good to be true—and yet it is! He tells how He sent His only Son to earth to win a bride, to transform her into a breathtaking beauty, and to one day take her to live with Him forever.

This love story is sometimes hidden and sometimes revealed, but it is the beat, beat, beat of His heart from Genesis to Revelation. He begins with a wedding (see Genesis 2:22–24), ends with a wedding (see Revelation 21:9–10), and threads this great love story through the poets, prophets, and parables. They all paint a picture of a *great* wedding day to come.

Even the very first miracle Jesus did was at a wedding—a miracle that for a long time mystified me. I thought, *Really, Lord? For Your first sign, You kept a party going? Why didn't You begin with something more stupendous, like stopping a storm or raising the dead?*

But I had completely missed the message He was sending! It makes perfect sense to me now that the first sign would be at a wedding. As we have seen in the Song, a wedding and the marriage that follows is the least inadequate metaphor for union and communion with Christ.

In the sixteenth century, Martin Luther turned to the Song for an illustration for his peers who were retreating from the gospel, feeling the permanency of the union depended on their works righteousness and trying to finish Christ's work by doing penance and paying indulgences.

So Luther expounded on the repeated refrain "I am my beloved's and my beloved is mine,"[2] emphasizing what we can know about our relationship with Christ from this picture of what happens when a man and woman are joined in holy matrimony. Everything that belonged to the bride now belongs to the groom, and everything that belonged to the groom now belongs to the bride.

So what do we, as the bride of Christ, give our Bridegroom?

Our shame.

Our sin.

Our brokenness.

And what does our Bridegroom give us?

His righteousness.

His mercy.

His riches.

How can this be? This is the great good news of the gospel! And this is the only truth that could live up to the title "Song of Songs," or the "Best of the Best." Earthly marriage can be wonderful, but it is not the best God has to give. Earthly vows can be broken, but God will never break His covenant with us. This is the great exchange of the gospel. This is the security of the covenant.

Likewise, that first sign at the wedding in John 2, of turning water into wine, was laden with rich symbolism. Philip Yancey writes, "Jesus, perhaps with a twinkle in his eye, transformed those jugs, ponderous symbols of the old way, into wineskins, harbingers of the new. . . . The time for ritual cleansing had passed; the time for celebration had begun."[3]

Do you see? The water represented religion. The wine represented the power and the passion of the gospel. And just as Jesus saved the best wine for the last (see

John 2:10), this Bridegroom whose "love is better than wine" (Song 1:2) has saved the best for the last in His Song of all Songs, with one poetic picture parading after another, thundering wonder into our hearts and firing our imaginations with the width, depth, and breadth of the love of our ultimate Bridegroom.

So hold on, here we go!

A Love Better Than Wine

The close of the Song brings us back to where we began, when the maiden was fantasizing about her wedding night, to the *dôd, dôd, dôd* of a boiling pot. In the opening of the Song, she said his love was better than wine, and now at the close—in reality and not in fantasy—he compares her breasts to clusters of the vine and her mouth to the very best wine. He tells her to let that wine flow smoothly over his lips (see Song 7:8–9). She tells him she will give him spiced wine to drink, the juice of her pomegranate (see Song 8:2–3). There is passion, there is pleasure, and there is the peaceful rest that follows lovemaking.

Amazingly, God uses this earthly picture of marriage and the marriage bed He designed to fire our imaginations for the deepest mystery, a mystery we can only glimpse through a glass darkly. Yet we know that one day we will experience a passion, a pleasure, and a peace beyond any bliss we've known on earth. Tim Keller says,

> The ecstasy and joy of sex is supposed to be a foretaste of the complete ecstasy and joy of total union with Christ. . . . The moment we see Him face to face there will be a closure, and yet a complete openness. We will be naked, and yet so delighted in, we will be unashamed.[4]

Why is marriage and the marriage bed such a perfect picture for the heart of Christianity? Because it points to what we need the most: union and communion with Christ. Being a Christian does not mean trying to be moral in our own strength but being transformed through union and communion with Christ.

The word *Christian* occurs only three times in Scripture, but the phrase *in Christ,* the concept of being in union and communion with Him, occurs around

165 times.[5] Could it be that God gave us this Song of all Songs to bring us back to the gospel, to the understanding that what matters most is abiding in Him and allowing this new wine of the Spirit to empower us throughout the day?

A RETURN TO EDEN

All through the Song we hear echoes of Eden, of the land that was lost, restored. Once again the flowers appear on the earth, the time of singing has come, and the voice of the turtledove is heard. It is a reverse of the Fall. Here, in the close, the bride says,

> I am my beloved's,
>> and his desire is for me.
>> —Song 7:10

This Hebrew word for "desire," *teshûqah,* occurs only two other times in the Bible, both in Genesis. It can mean sexual desire, as when God told Eve,

> I will surely multiply your pain in childbearing;
>> in pain you shall bring forth children.
> Your desire shall be contrary to your husband,
>> but he shall rule over you.
>> —Genesis 3:16

And it can also mean the desire to control, as when God warned Cain,

> Sin is crouching at the door. Its desire is contrary to you, but you must rule over it.
>> —Genesis 4:7

In the proclaiming of the curse, it very well may mean both, for despite pain in childbirth, a woman will desire a man sexually, and when he desires to dominate her, she will respond with a desire to dominate him. Discord has replaced harmony—both in marriage and in man's relationship with God.

But the picture at the close of the Song is of harmony restored, and "the reconciliation pictured here will be *as far reaching as the curse has been.*"[6] This is the day that "Joy to the World" sings of—not of Jesus's first coming, but of His second coming!

> No more let sins and sorrows grow,
> nor thorns infest the ground;
> He comes to make His blessings flow
> Far as the curse is found
> far as the curse is found
> far as, far as, the curse is found.[7]

SAVING THE BEST FOR LAST

When Steve was dying, I told him I wanted to be like widows in pagan countries who were burned on the pyre with their husband's body. I couldn't imagine life ever being sweet again.

Never did I imagine that what I feared most in this life would actually press me into God so deeply that He would turn my mourning into dancing. But He has. He has brought me up out of the wilderness, and my cup overflows with joy.

This is where the Shulammite is: filled with joy and gratitude, remembering the bridegroom's many mercies to her, such as how he awakened her under the apple tree (see Song 8:5), how he has married her and carried her through the wilderness. As we mature in Christ, we can look back and reflect on how He has carried us from the womb to our old age (see Isaiah 46:3–4). That reality can produce the best fruit in our vineyard, the best wine from our grapes.

How sweet it is to watch an elderly couple so deeply in love that you know that many waters cannot quench that love—not wrinkles, not walkers, not waning minds.

My dear friend and mentor Win Couchman has had a long and beautiful marriage to Bob. But after seventy-two years of marriage, Bob lost his memory and Win lost the physical strength to give him the care he needed. So they faced the day when Bob was to be moved to a care facility. Win called it "Move Bob Away from Win Day." In a magazine for pastors' wives, Win wrote,

Scary. Yet as the time got closer, God was faithful to show me new pictures from His Word. The Wedding at Cana. The whole business of the wedding celebration running out of wine, and Jesus casually turning huge containers of water into the best wine of the day. Over and over God reassured me that He would make this season of our lives His best wine.

After Bob moved into the care facility, Win went to his airy dining room to have Sunday noontime dinner with him. Then she walked him back to his room. He was weary, and he flopped on the bed while she read beside him:

> Suddenly I was given an inspiration. I said, "Honey, would you like it if I took off my shoes and crawled up there beside you?" Bob shouted, "I would love it!"
>
> The minute I lay down beside him, he put his arms around me, put his head on my shoulder, and went sound asleep. Then I understood how God was going to turn the water of our move into His best wine. Every time I visit Bob, we eat together, then walk back to his new home. I lie down beside him, he puts his arms around me, and we are once more completely what we have been all these years: two people who love each other with all their hearts and are free to spend the next half hour in each other's arms. Nothing to do but relax into the pattern of a good old marriage.[8]

In the same way, in a spiritual relationship with Christ, as you, by faith, die to yourself and surrender to Him, your relationship deepens into an intimacy you may never have dreamed could be possible—and the fruitfulness of your life increases dramatically, with the best grapes, the best wine.

You can see this on an individual level, but oh my, how you can see this on a corporate level as well. Richard Wurmbrand, who was tortured and imprisoned for fourteen years for his faith in Communist Romania, wrote two books on the Song of Songs filled with testimonies from those who were persecuted for Christ in Communist countries. Many of those saints eventually were martyred. Yet, Wurmbrand says that "amidst their torment they retained their joy. . . . This is why the blood of the martyrs became the seed of the church."[9] One day I imagine those martyrs going with Christ into the vineyards to see the thousands in heaven that sprang up from the seed of their blood. Christ is saving the best wine for last.

THE STRENGTH OF LOVE

Many commentators believe that the following passage ended the original Song, and that is possible. They are perhaps the most famous words in the Song:

> Set me as a seal upon your heart,
>   as a seal upon your arm,
> for love is strong as death,
>   jealousy is fierce as the grave.
> Its flashes are flashes of fire,
>   the very flame of the LORD.
> Many waters cannot quench love,
>   neither can floods drown it.
>   —Song of Songs 8:6–7

These words are spoken at earthly weddings, and beautifully so, for we need the Spirit of God to help us keep our covenant of forsaking all others and being true in sickness and in health, for richer or for poorer, and for better or for worse. Here in the Song, the wedding has already happened and she is his. Yet she knows he is going away. He must leave her now and she must remain true until he returns—and she does not know when that will be. She knows that her heart is prone to wander, so she asks him to set her as a seal upon his heart, like the old hymn "Come Thou Fount" pleads:

> Let Thy goodness, like a fetter,
> Bind my wandering heart to Thee:
> Prone to wander, Lord, I feel it,
> Prone to leave the God I love;
> Here's my heart, O take and seal it;
> Seal it for Thy courts above.[10]

The bride goes on to say that "love is strong as death." Anyone who has seen a parent, spouse, or child in a coffin knows the strength of death. Yet in our denial stage of grief, we may imagine the loved one coming back to us. When I was telling my grief counselor that I just couldn't give Steve's clothes away, she pierced my heart with the reality I needed: "Dee, he's not coming back."

Death is strong—but God's love is stronger. In fact, *His* love will overcome death. God showed this to one of the earliest men who ever lived: Job. In his misery, Job pleads for death but then suddenly, in fear, asks God,

> If a man dies, shall he live again?
> —Job 14:14

The Spirit of the living God comes to Job, showing him that His love has the power to overcome death. In a flash of light, Job exclaims,

> You will call and I will answer you;
> > you will long for the creature your hands
> > > have made.
> —Job 14:15, NIV

Just as Jesus missed Lazarus, for His hands made him, and just as He called Lazarus by name to rise from the dead, one day Jesus will call your name and my name and the names of all who are in Him, who are set as a seal on His heart—and they *will* rise with new resurrection bodies to be with Him forevermore.

The Song continues with more bold images of God's love for us:

> Its flashes are flashes of fire,
> > the very flame of the LORD.
> —Song 8:6

God's love for us is never lukewarm; it is *hot.* My young friend Amy, who has been struggling to believe the simplicity of the gospel—the fact that her debt has been paid *in full* by another—was outside watching men burn branches at a bonfire on their farm. As the flames leaped into the air, she sensed the Spirit of the Lord saying, *That's how intense My love is for you.*

God *is* jealous for us, for He knows how running to false lovers can destroy us. His jealousy is as "fierce as the grave" (Song 8:6). When we understand the passion God has for us, it can help us surrender our idols to Him, whether our idols take the form of over-working, over-controlling, or over-obsessing. We can let go and trust Him to meet us!

I have a dear friend who is the mother of four sons. Her eldest, a teenager, has decided he doesn't believe in God. She said, "Before I understood heart idols, I would have tried to control him, continually debating with him, hovering over him. But because of the Song, I have a greater trust that God is jealous for my son and that instead of my trying to 'fix' him, it is far better for me to simply pray, love, and release him to my wise and wonderful God."

MANY WATERS

When I was speaking to women at an African American church, endeavoring to encourage them in the midst of their suffering, they turned the tables and encouraged me.

From the pulpit I began to quote the end of Romans 8 to them, saying, "Who shall separate us from the love of Christ? . . . For I am sure that neither death nor life—"

And before I could continue, a woman cried out, "Nor angels, nor principalities, nor powers!"

And I thought, *Oh my, I hope I know this—and I hope I know it in the King James Version!* I said, "Nor things present, nor things to come."

They clapped, they cheered, and then they chimed back, "Nor height, nor depth."

And I said, "Nor any other creature."

And we finished together: "Shall be able to separate us from the love of God, which is in Christ Jesus our Lord."

Because most of these women had experienced far greater suffering than I had, I knew that they had these promises hidden in their hearts, promises that had sustained them when the waters of prejudice, hate, and injustice roared. They knew, firsthand,

> Many waters cannot quench love,
>   neither can floods drown it.
> —Song 8:7

This truth is one we must cling to, for Jesus warned us of increasing persecution in the last days, before He returns. How greatly has persecution against Christians accelerated in the past decade, and we must remember that no matter what comes, He is with us and nothing, absolutely nothing, can quench His love.

ONE WHO FINDS PEACE

The closing chapter of the Song speaks of "a little sister" who "is a wall" (desiring to preserve her virginity). But the Shulammite proudly declares,

> I was a wall,
>   and my breasts were like towers;
> then I was in his eyes
>   as one who finds peace.
> —Song 8:10

This has both an earthly and a spiritual application. How pleased is the husband who has a virginal bride (and the wife who has a virginal husband)! I realize this is a rare gift today. Yet in Christ, amazingly, we can become virgins again. Consider how Jesus responded to those with sexually immoral pasts, such as the Samaritan woman who'd had five husbands (see John 4) and the adulterous woman who wept at His feet (see Luke 7). He never shamed them but cleansed them. His blood has the power to make us white as snow.

Spiritually, this theme should ring several bells. Paul told the Corinthians not to listen to false teachers so that he could present them "as a pure virgin to Christ" (2 Corinthians 11:2). There is also a spiritual symbolism in the white wedding garment: it represents being clothed in the righteousness of Christ (see the parable in

Matthew 22:11–13 of the man who tried to get in *without* a wedding garment). Likewise, we keep our garment clean by keeping short accounts and by repenting as soon as we soil it, for He will be "faithful and just to forgive us our sins and to cleanse us from all unrighteousness" (1 John 1:9). As we do these things, we will be in His eyes "as one who finds peace" (Song 8:10).

When I guard my mind against false teaching, which comes mostly through mass media, when I walk in the light as He is in the light, confessing my sin whenever I step into the darkness, I am enveloped by His love and the peace of His presence. Nothing compares to that, which is why the bridegroom says,

> If a man offered for love
>> all the wealth of his house,
>> he would be utterly despised.
> —Song 8:7

We must not be like Esau, who sold his birthright for a bowl of stew. We must cherish the gospel, this pearl of great price, and be willing, if God calls us to do so, to give everything to keep it. I cannot help but think of our brothers and sisters in Syria and neighboring lands who are giving up *everything* but this pearl in the face of persecution. They have given up their countries, their homes, and their very lives for Christ. The one thing they will never give up is their faith.

COME, LORD JESUS!

The Song closes, not with the lovers walking hand and hand into their happily ever after, but with a dose of reality. The beloved must leave again, but this time it is his decision, not because she has turned him away. There is grief, but not grief without hope.

When the disciples were grieving because Jesus told them He was going away, He said,

> Let not your hearts be troubled. Believe in God; believe also in me. In
> my Father's house are many rooms. If it were not so, would I have told
> you that I go to prepare a place for you? And if I go and prepare a place

for you, I will come again and will take you to myself, that where I am
you may be also.
—John 14:1–3

Jesus has wooed us and won us, and one amazing day He *is* coming back to
wed us. The closing words in the Song are a poignant call for the groom to return:

Make haste, my beloved,
    and be like a gazelle
or a young stag
    on the mountains of spices.
—Song 8:14

In the same way, the book of Revelation closes with the bride calling,

Come, Lord Jesus!
—Revelation 22:20

As Charles Spurgeon says, "The Song of love and the Book of love end in almost the self same way, with a strong desire for Christ's speedy return."[11]

When Satan condemns you with your failures, when he tells you that God
couldn't love you, do not fear. You are washed and dressed in a robe of righteousness. God looks at you and says,

You are altogether beautiful, my love;
    there is no flaw in you.
—Song 4:7

Do you believe that God sees you as altogether beautiful? That His banner over
you is love? This is the refrain to return to again and again. Confidence in God's
love will cause the devil to flee, the troubles of this world to make you stronger, and
joy to fill your heart like the joy of a beloved bride on her wedding day.

This is the Song above all Songs—for what song could be better than this?

LESSON 12: SONG OF SONGS 8:1–14

 Icebreaker

Has this book and study helped the love of God move more deeply into your heart? If so, share a specific passage from the Song that was particularly helpful and explain why.

Memory Work

Instead of memory work this week, take a day to read all the way through the Song on your own and write down a few things to share in your group that stand out to you about the Song as a whole.

Read Chapter 12 of *He Calls You Beautiful*

1. What two things stood out to you the most?

Prepare your heart for study with Danny Byram's song "I Must Leave You Now."[12]

2. The Bible is not a series of stories but one story. The gospel is like a multifaceted prism: every time it turns, we see new colors, new beauty. In every book of the Bible, I see the gospel from another angle and it pierces my heart. Explain how each of the following stories, from many different genres, fits into the big story.

   a. Genesis 2:22–24 along with Ephesians 5:31–32

b. Psalm 45 (Jonathan Edwards called this the Song in a nutshell)

c. The Song of Songs

d. Hosea 2:14–20

e. Matthew 22:1–14

f. Revelation 19:6–9

3. When you see how God's love story beats through all of Scripture, what insight does this give you into the Song? How does it impact you?

4. Read Song 7:6–10. Find pictures that speak of passion, pleasure, and peace.

*5. Have you experienced passion, pleasure, and peace in your relationship with the Lord? If so, give specific examples for as many as you can.

6. Read Song 7:11–13 and note pictures of fruitfulness.

*7. The heart of Christianity is union and communion with Christ. How is the fruitfulness of the vineyard in the Song similar to the metaphor in John 15:4–5? What fruitfulness do you see in your life?

8. Read Song 8:1–4. What refrain is repeated here, and what is significant about it?

9. Read Song 8:5. How has the wilderness experience caused the bride to grow? How has it caused you to grow? Be specific.

10. Read Song 8:6–7 slowly. (This is another passage that is valuable to memorize.) Take just one of the pictures and comment on why it is meaningful to you.

11. The bride has the sense that her beloved is about to leave, so she asks to be set as a seal upon his heart. Review the lyrics from "Come Thou Fount," and then explain why this is a good prayer.

12. Why does the Lord have a right to be jealous for us? Of what do you think He is jealous in your life?

13. Have you grown to the point in your intimacy with the Lord that many waters cannot quench this love? If so, what does this look like?

14. What should be done for the little sister who is a wall? A door? What might this mean both on an earthly and a spiritual level?

15. What contrast do you see between Song 1:6 and Song 8:11–12? What is the significance of that difference?

16. The shepherd-king is leaving, so what does his bride tell him in Song 8:14? Compare this to Revelation 22:17, 20. What do you see?

17. What has been the impact of the Song on your relationship with Jesus? If you are married, how has it impacted your earthly marriage?

ᴗ Prayer Time

Prepare for the final prayer time together by taking a concept or verse that has been meaningful to you and pray it in thanksgiving or in intercession for yourself and the other women in the group. For example:

- *Lord, I thank You that You are jealous for me, that You come running for me, that Your banner over me is love.*
- *Lord, help us reflect You as the moon reflects the sun. Help us be like an army with banners!*

Facilitator Resources

Hints for Group Facilitators

Your role is crucial in helping women feel appreciated and in keeping the group discussion lively! Here are some tried-and-true hints.

Keep the homework bar high. If group members don't have their books ahead of time, do the Get-Acquainted Lesson together on the spot and then assign the first chapter and first lesson to be done the next week. Explain that though they don't have to be mature Christians to do this study, they do need to be motivated enough to do the homework. The Song is too challenging to understand without study—and also, since the *point* of the Song is intimacy with Jesus, they must spend time with Him!

The links provided throughout the book will greatly enhance their study. Let them know that if a link doesn't work, the videos can be found at www.deebrestin.com /hecallsyoubeautiful.

Keep the ball rolling. Most important: Don't teach; facilitate! You want to hear from the group members, so if they ask you a question, throw it back to the group. Watch facial expressions to draw out quieter members. Go around the whole group when you're asking icebreaker and takeaway questions, giving freedom to pass. Don't be afraid of silences—introverts need pauses to gather courage. If the silence seems very long, rephrase the question.

Help monopolizers hold back. If monopolizing is a problem, remind the group to allow silences so others can gather courage to speak up. Try to sit next to rather than across from a monopolizer because eye contact encourages sharing. If the problem persists, speak gently one on one to the offender. Affirm her contributions and ask her to help by holding back and giving others time to gather courage to speak up.

Start on time and end on time. If you don't, you encourage tardiness and discourage those who have to be out on time from coming at all.

Communicate often. Social media makes this easier. Encourage group members individually, remind them of the next meeting, and let absentees know they were missed!

Affirm answers. A nod, a smile, saying "That's good!" or "That's interesting!"—all of these help encourage participation. (Even off-the-wall comments can be interesting. If it is a dangerously wrong answer, don't pounce, but ask what someone else thinks or direct the group back to the text.) People need to feel appreciated and welcome or they will drop out.

Pray! Each week for each member. This is vital.

Get-Acquainted Lesson

Getting to Know One Another

1. Go around the circle and share your name along with an adjective about you that begins with the same letter as the first letter in your name (such as Nurse Nancy or Shy Sherri). Before you share your name, say the names of everyone who has already spoken.

2. Have you ever done a Bible study before? If so, what did you like about it? What do you hope to gain from this study?

*3. Your facilitator will pass around a spool of thread. Break off as much as you want. Then she will tell you what to do with it.

Getting a Glimpse of the Song of Songs

4. The Song of Songs is a poetic love song, and poetry is always multilayered. For this reason, you need to be open to both earthly and spiritual meanings in the text. For example, consider:

He will cover you with his feathers,
   and under his wings you will find refuge.
   —Psalm 91:4, NIV

a. What is the earthly picture in this verse? How does it shed light on the spiritual picture of God and a believer?

b. How might you misinterpret Psalm 91:4 if you saw *only* the earthly picture?

c. The Song of Songs is an earthly picture of the love of a bridegroom for his bride and her responsive love to him. This points to a spiritual picture. Read Ephesians 5:31–32 and explain what mystery marriage foreshadows.

5. Read out loud Song of Songs 1:1–4.

a. On an earthly level, how can you see the euphoria of the first-love time?

b. On a spiritual level, the Song is meant to awaken our senses with its word pictures. This is not an allegory where a kiss represents just one thing, such as answered prayer. A kiss represents many ways that Jesus comes to you, such as through His Word, His Spirit, and divinely timed circumstances. With this in mind, can you think of some ways you have been kissed by the King? If so, share one.

c. Can you share one way Jesus's love has been better than wine to you?

d. Share any observations you have on verses 1–4. (Even if you have questions and not answers, that will help stir your desire to read more for next week.)

6. Some Bible study groups are richer than others. With this in mind, ponder these questions:

a. Why do you think a group is richer when individuals come prepared with their homework? What helps motivate you to get your homework done?

b. Some people talk easily, and some need long pauses to gather courage to speak up. Which of those describes you? If you're talkative, how could you help the shy members? If you're shy, how might you decide ahead of time when you might speak up?

c. What else do you think makes a rich group? How could you help?

Together, watch the thirteen-minute online video from theologian and author Mike Reeves titled "Enjoying Christ Constantly."[1] (Facilitators, if possible, plug a laptop into a larger screen.) Afterward everyone should share comments as they feel led.

Before you meet next week, read chapter 1 in this book, highlighting things that stand out to you. Then complete lesson 1. Do a little each day.

Lesson-by-Lesson Leader Notes

Answers to questions can be found in the Bible text or in the chapter text, but in this section, you'll find help for some of the more challenging questions, which are marked in each lesson with an asterisk (*).

Get-Acquainted Lesson (Optional)

3. Pass around a spool of thread and tell them to break off any amount. Then tell them to wind their thread around one of their fingers and tell the group things that will help others get to know them (what they love, what a typical day looks like, what they know about the Song of Songs, and so on) until the thread is completely wrapped.

Hook up someone's laptop or iPad to a TV screen if possible, unless your group is small enough to gather around a laptop. Watch the thirteen-minute online video from Mike Reeves titled "Enjoying Christ Constantly" and then invite people to share their reactions.[1]

Lesson 1: The Best Song of All

Pass around a sheet of paper and have each woman list her contact information and the best way to be reached (text, e-mail, Facebook?). During the week, make copies to hand out at the next meeting.

Depending on your time and group size, you may need to skip some questions. Circle ones you definitely want to answer, and then pace the discussion. If conversation regarding a particular question becomes lively, deep, and edifying, let the group members linger, for the Spirit is moving. Better to miss some questions than to quench the Spirit.

Remember to be the facilitator and not the teacher. The participants—not you—should do most of the talking.

If this is the first time you've met, then this week watch and discuss the thirteen-minute online video from Mike Reeves titled "Enjoying Christ Constantly."[2] (Some may have watched it at home, but some will not have. Either way, this video is an important introduction to the Song, and repetition never hurts.)

6. You might ask follow-up questions, such as, what do you think it is about the marriage relationship that foreshadows Christ and His bride? On the husband's part? On the wife's part? On becoming one?

8b and 9b. You may need to prime the pump by being vulnerable yourself or asking a mature woman in the group to be.

11. Always go around the group with the takeaway question, giving individuals freedom to pass.

Prayer Time: Model this with three mature women. Explain that they will have already shared their prayer requests with one another and that now you are going to facilitate the prayer. Have them do the same in small groups; members of each group will need to appoint a facilitator. For example:

You/Facilitator: Let's pray for Debbie.
Vicki: Please help Debbie get in the habit of meeting with You each morning.
Jan: Give her a longing for this.
You: Let's pray for Vicki . . .

After you meet, you might e-mail the links to two additional sets of video messages. (See endnotes for more information.) Also, these would be wonderful enrichment for you as the facilitator.[3]

Lesson 2: Poetry to Penetrate Our Hearts

5b. gentleness, strength, beauty, swiftness to appear and disappear
5c. love-cooing, gentleness, peacefulness, timidity, focus
6b. Moses leading God's people out of slavery is a picture of Christ's redemption; David suffered, but Psalm 22 goes beyond that to what Christ suffered; Isaiah prophesies specifics about Christ's crucifixion.

14. Members' opinions might vary on which picture is most important (marriage or Christ). Assure them that's fine. Both are there, so they will learn from both. My opinion is that Jesus is preeminent, but they are free to disagree and express why.

Lesson 3: Kiss Me

Be sure you have the group members pair off to do their memory work (Song 2:10–11 for this week) and share thoughts. If they got off to a bad start, tell them they have another week to get it right and they will be so enriched by doing it. The memory passage from the English Standard Version is in the back of this book.

3. Reading aloud and allowing them to share thoughts is a wonderful way to broaden the discussion beyond the questions, so don't skip these questions.

4. Christianity is not rules and rituals but relationship—intimacy with God.

9. Aaron and Miriam thought God had spoken to them, but God clarified they had missed it and that He had spoken directly to Moses ("mouth to mouth"). So with this in mind, a kiss on the mouth could represent very clear communication from God.

13. If group members need help, direct them to Matthew 1:21 and Matthew 1:23; then ask why the meaning of these names might bring comfort, as oil does.

14. The Song is about both the individual and the corporate bride.

Lesson 4: Dark, but Lovely

Remember to have the group members pair off for memory work of Song 2:10–11.

If you want to do "secret sisters," this might be a good week to start it. Have members draw names from a hat. They can send notes, little gifts, and pray for their secret sister during the weeks you meet together. Then you can reveal the names at your final gathering—perhaps at a special luncheon. If women are absent, make sure they are included if they want to be. And keep track of who has whom!

5c. We still have sinful hearts, yet we are covered in the righteousness of Christ.

7d. You may need to get things going by being vulnerable.

10. If group members need help, refer to the story of Annie. What helped her admit her wrong? What helped her carry out her repentance? Then ask how they might apply this to a besetting sin in their own lives, such as surrendering to anger or anxiety.

Lesson 5: The Apple Tree and the Lily

9d. This may be controversial, even among believers today. You can set the tone by saying, "We might disagree, but we can share our convictions and why we hold them scripturally. We should speak once in love, listen to everyone carefully, and then move on."

Lesson 6: Come Away, My Love!

E-mail individual encouragement to group members during the week. We all need to feel appreciated!

8c. It's so easy to be content with being saved from the penalty of sin and not want to press on to be saved from the power of sin as well. Yet we are deceiving ourselves, for sin is never our friend.

Lesson 7: I Sought the One My Soul Loves

10c. Song 3:6 and 5:10

10d. Song 3:11

10e. Song 2:10 and 2:13 (many believe this is a marriage proposal)

10f. Ask for descriptions of the bride from the Song that show her glorious character (one is Song 6:10)

10g. Song 3:11

10h. Song 1:3

Lesson 8: An Oasis in the Wilderness

4. goats in Gilead; God blessed Jacob, and his sheep bore twins; Rahab's scarlet thread led to her rescue; David's tower is famous in Jerusalem; and the mountain of myrrh implies sacrifice such as occurred in the temple in Jerusalem

Lesson 9: The Lukewarm Bride

If you have singles in your group, you might ask them to share their unique perspective on this chapter. How does it impact them?

Lesson 10: The Fairest of Ten Thousand

4. Frightening vs. altogether lovely; dead vs. alive; feet of clay vs. feet of gold

Lesson 11: The Dancing Shulammite

You may want to plan a special meal for next week, your last session; remind everyone that secret sisters will be revealed!

5. Ecstatic experiences, while not the norm, can happen. You may or may not want to take the time to see if anyone has experienced such ecstasy or was moved by one of the accounts in the chapter.
6. As we fill our minds with things of the Lord, returning to His rest will happen naturally. But we can also be intentional about listening to music and good sermons and setting our affections on things above.
7. She has been refined through her time in the wilderness and has the maturity to bring peace.

Lesson 12: The Best Is Yet to Come

If you are having a special meal, you could share the icebreaker and a passage that meant a lot. You can also take time to bless one another. Lift up the name of each woman and have just a few share a reason they appreciate her.

5. If the group is stumped, add these questions: Has God given you a passion to serve Him in any way or a passion to know Him better? Has God delighted you with surprising circumstances or an answer to prayer? Has God given you His peace in the midst of challenging circumstances?
7. Remind them it isn't prideful to see growth, for it comes from God.

Song of Songs 2:10–17

My beloved speaks and says to me:
"Arise, my love, my beautiful one,
  and come away,
for behold, the winter is past;
  the rain is over and gone.
The flowers appear on the earth,
  the time of singing has come,
and the voice of the turtledove
  is heard in our land.
The fig tree ripens its figs,
  and the vines are in blossom;
  they give forth fragrance.
Arise, my love, my beautiful one,
  and come away.
O my dove, in the clefts of the rock,
  in the crannies of the cliff,
let me see your face,
  let me hear your voice,
for your voice is sweet,
  and your face is lovely.
Catch the foxes for us,
  the little foxes
that spoil the vineyards,
  for our vineyards are in blossom."

My beloved is mine, and I am his;
  he grazes among the lilies.
Until the day breathes
  and the shadows flee,
turn, my beloved, be like a gazelle
  or a young stag on cleft mountains.

Acknowledgments

My Editor, Elisa Fryling Stanford

You've always been amazing as we've worked together with past books, but this time I truly believe you *made* this book a work of beauty. "The purposes of a man's heart are deep waters, but a man of understanding draws them out" (Proverbs 20:5, NIV). When I talked around a passage because I thought it too challenging, you pressed, you asked questions—until you drew out truth I didn't even know I had. When *you* didn't understand something, I knew I had to go back and make it clearer. It is amazing to me just how clear the deep waters of the Song have become. I pray its truth ripples out to His bride so she can see just how loved she is.

Early Readers

Even when I was hovering over the waters of the deep and made early fumbling attempts to express what I was seeing, there were a few who plodded through what I'd written, encouraging me that there was gold here. In particular, I thank Linda Strom, Rebecca Dority, Lizzy and Jon Richardson, Sylvia Spencer, Ann Dahl, and the women who went through my Bible studies using the blog on my website.

My Faithful Praying Friends

Your unseen labor is not in vain, for I know I have been quickened because of your faithful prayers.

The Team at WaterBrook Multnomah

I'm so thankful to God for leading me to you. Liz Curtis Higgs raved about you, and Linda Strom said, "They have had a heart for ministry—how they have helped our prison ministry." I'd been told the Song was too deep for today's Christian women, but when Laura Barker called me, she said you wanted this manuscript because it was deep. Already you have shown your heart for prison ministry by promising so many books for them. Thanks so for listening to me and for allowing me to work with Elisa. Ginia Hairston Croker, Lisa Beech, and Laura Wright have all been a delight. I appreciate all those behind the scenes at WaterBrook Multnomah who serve for God's glory.

Dr. Michael Reeves and Dr. Ellen F. Davis
There might be more commentaries on the Song of Songs than any Old Testament book, but these two contemporary theologians are particularly illuminating in their insights on the Song. Rather than interpreting the Song as either just about marriage or just about Christ, they hold both pictures side by side and see so much more. I am indebted to each of them. I know my readers would be blessed by getting Dr. Davis's commentary and listening to Dr. Reeves's teaching on the Song of Songs online. (Find this information at www.deebrestin.com/hecallsyoubeautiful.)

Notes

Chapter 1: The Best Song of All

1. "Mike Reeves—Enjoying Christ Constantly," YouTube video, 13:31, posted by "WelcomeToTheSermon," May 2, 2013, www.youtube.com/watch?v=NRH_E2u5cGY.
2. "Audio Bible Book of Song of Songs, Chapters 1–8," YouTube video, 20:15, posted by "Lowman Whitfield," May 30, 2011, www.youtube.com/watch?v=r6uEgKpzqOo; turn on the captions to see the Scripture.

Chapter 2: Poetry to Penetrate Our Hearts

1. Mike Mason, *The Mystery of Marriage: As Iron Sharpens Iron* (Colorado Springs, CO: Multnomah, 1985), 43.
2. Derek Kidner, *The Message of Hosea* (Leicester, England: InterVarsity, 1980), 33.
3. Mike Reeves, "The Love of Christ in the Song of Songs 1," Union Resources audio, 54:20, www.uniontheology.org/resources/bible/old-testament/the-love-of-christ-in-the-song-of-songs-1.
4. See www.deebrestin.com.
5. Sally Lloyd-Jones, *The Jesus Storybook Bible: Every Story Whispers His Name* (Grand Rapids, MI: Zonderkidz, 2007), 17.
6. Wilson H. Kimnach, ed., *Jonathan Edwards: Sermons and Discourses, 1720–1723,* vol. 10 of *The Works of Jonathan Edwards,* ed. John E. Smith (New Haven, CT, and London: Yale University Press, 1992), 154–5.
7. "Mike Reeves—Enjoying Christ Constantly," YouTube video, 13:31, posted by "WelcomeToTheSermon," May 2, 2013, www.youtube.com/watch?v=NRH_E2u5cGY.
8. "Mike Reeves—Enjoying Christ Constantly."
9. Ellen F. Davis, *Proverbs, Ecclesiastes, and the Song of Songs* (Louisville, KY: Westminster John Knox, 2000), 239–40, 271.
10. Mike Reeves, "Sibbes: The Love of Christ 1," *The Love of Christ in Song of Songs,* Theology Network audio, 54:20, www.theologynetwork.org/unquenchable-flame/the-reformation-in-britain/the-love-of-christ-in-song-of-songs.htm.
11. "The Song of Solomon," Ligonier Ministries, www.ligonier.org/learn/devotionals/song-solomon.
12. Cyril of Alexandria, quoted in Iain M. Duguid, *Song of Songs,* Reformed Expository Commentary (Phillipsburg, NJ: P&R, 2016), 25.

13. Stephen J. Stein, ed., *Jonathan Edwards: Notes on Scripture,* vol. 15 of *The Works of Jonathan Edwards,* ed. John E. Smith (New Haven, CT, and London: Yale University Press, 1998), 547.

14. Davis, *Proverbs,* 237.

15. Richard Sibbes, *The Love of Christ* (1639; repr., Edinburgh, UK: Banner of Truth Trust, 2011), 1.

16. C. S. Lewis, *God in the Dock* (New York: Eerdmans, 2014), 292; emphasis added.

17. Michael Card, quoted in Dee Brestin, *Idol Lies: Facing the Truth About Our Deepest Desires* (Brentwood, TN: Worthy, 2012), 65.

18. James M. Hamilton Jr., "Why You Need to Preach the Song of Songs," *For His Renown* (blog), September 21, 2015, http://jimhamilton.info/2015/09/21/why-you-need-to-preach-the-song-of-songs.

19. "'Song of Solomon' from Martin Smith (Official Lyric Video)," YouTube video, 6:26, posted by "integritymusic," November 3, 2014, www.youtube.com/watch?v=zyIR4N5EFt8.

Chapter 3: Kiss Me

1. Tim and Kathy Keller, "The Meaning of Marriage," Let's Strengthen Marriage, webinar, November 1, 2011, www.marriagewebinar.org/mw4/view.htm.

2. John Eldredge, *The Journey of Desire: Searching for the Life We've Only Dreamed Of* (Grand Rapids, MI: Zondervan, 2000), 35.

3. George Mueller, quoted in Paul E. Little, *How to Give Away Your Faith* (Downers Grove, IL: InterVarsity, 2008), 178.

4. Jamie Lash, quoted in Jamie L. Perez, *The Perpetual Flame: Offering Acceptable Worship unto God* (Lincoln: NE: iUniverse, 2001), 163.

5. Ellen F. Davis, *Proverbs, Ecclesiastes, and the Song of Songs* (Louisville, KY: Westminster John Knox, 2000), 231.

6. Davis, *Proverbs,* 231.

7. James M. Hamilton Jr., *Song of Songs* (Glasgow, UK: Christian Focus, 2015), 15.

8. "On the Persecuted Church: Panel with Nancy Guthrie, Mindy Belz, Don Carson, K. A. Ellis, Nastaran Farahani," Vimeo video, 58:25, posted by "The Gospel Coalition," June 18, 2016, https://vimeo.com/171214572.

9. Marilynne Robinson, *Home: A Novel* (New York: Farrar, Straus, and Giroux, 2008), 104.

10. Michael V. Fox, *The Song of Songs and the Ancient Egyptian Love Songs* (Madison, WI: University of Wisconsin Press, 1985), 109.

Chapter 4: Dark, but Lovely

1. "*Scent of a Woman* Tango Scene," YouTube video, 4:30, posted by "CabasseAlbatros," June 4, 2013, www.youtube.com/watch?v=eTaxHav5mww.

2. Brent Curtis and John Eldredge, *The Sacred Romance: Drawing Closer to the Heart of God* (Nashville: Thomas Nelson, 1997), 20.

3. Lauren F. Winner, *Girl Meets God: On the Path to a Spiritual Life* (Chapel Hill, NC: Algonquin, 2002), 57.

4. Sara Groves and Nat Sabin, "Maybe There's a Loving God," *All Right Here,* Integrity Media, 2002.

5. We did my seeker study *Examining the Claims of Jesus: Answers to Your Questions About Christ* (Colorado Springs, CO: WaterBrook, 1985); Rebecca Pippert also has two excellent seeker studies.

6. Tim Keller, *Gospel in Life Study Guide: Grace Changes Everything* (Grand Rapids, MI: Zondervan, 2010), 16.

7. Ellen F. Davis, *Proverbs, Ecclesiastes, and the Song of Songs* (Louisville, KY: Westminster John Knox, 2000), 243.

8. Davis, *Proverbs,* 245.

9. Thomas Moore, *Care of the Soul: A Guide for Cultivating Depth and Sacredness in Everyday Life* (San Francisco: HarperCollins, 1992), 263.

10. "Nothing but the Blood—Matt Redman," YouTube video, 6:28, posted by "Greg Rice," June 22, 2007, www.youtube.com/watch?v=UtsxdtEN_G4.

Chapter 5: The Apple Tree and the Lily

1. Ellen F. Davis, *Proverbs, Ecclesiastes, and the Song of Songs* (Louisville, KY: Westminster John Knox, 2000), 247.

2. Neil Warren and Richard Mouw, "Overworked and Looking for Love," Gospel in Life, June 1, 2012, www.gospelinlife.com/sermons/overworked-looking-for-love -8247.html.

3. Mike Mason, *The Mystery of Marriage: As Iron Sharpens Iron* (Colorado Springs, CO: Multnomah, 1985), 37.

4. Paul Tournier, *The Gift of Feeling* (Louisville, KY: Knox, 1981), 27.

5. Davis, *Proverbs,* 250.

6. Mason, *Mystery of Marriage,* 43.

7. Davis, *Proverbs,* 248.

8. "Blaise Pascal: Scientific and Spiritual Prodigy," Christian History, *Christianity Today,* www.christianitytoday.com/ch/131christians/evangelistsandapologists /pascal.html.

9. John Piper, "Dwight L. Moody Turns 172," *Desiring God,* February 5, 2009, www .desiringgod.org/blog/posts/dwight-l-moody-turns-172.

10. Warren and Mouw, "Overworked and Looking for Love."

11. "Dove's Eyes," YouTube video, 2:32, posted by "Misty Edwards—Topic," November 21, 2014, www.youtube.com/watch?v=muQL4-N8_I8&list=PLTHVamh _JeShr8jq-G9LQWWYCi0sVq2Mf&index=15.

Chapter 6: Come Away, My Love!

1. J. R. R. Tolkien, quoted in Humphrey Carpenter, *J. R. R. Tolkien: A Biography* (Boston: Houghton Mifflin, 2000), 151.
2. John of the Cross, *The Collected Works of St. John of the Cross*, trans. K. Kavanaugh and O. Rodriguez (Washington, DC: ICS, 1991), 484.
3. Larry Crabb, *Soul Talk: The Language God Longs for Us to Speak* (Nashville: Thomas Nelson, 2003), 69.
4. Barbara Duguid, *Extravagant Grace: God's Glory Displayed in Our Weakness* (Phillipsburg, NJ: P&R, 2013), 37–43.
5. Ellen F. Davis, *Proverbs, Ecclesiastes, and the Song of Songs* (Louisville, KY: Westminster John Knox, 2000), 251.
6. Iain M. Duguid, *Song of Songs*, Reformed Expository Commentary (Phillipsburg, NJ: P&R, 2016), 43.
7. Walter Trobisch, *I Married You* (New York, Harper & Row: 1971), 13.
8. Trobisch, *I Married You*, 15.
9. David Barshinger, *Jonathan Edwards and the Psalms* (Oxford: Oxford University Press, 2014), 179–80.
10. C. S. Lewis, *Mere Christianity* (New York: HarperOne, 2015), 53.
11. Rankin Wilbourne, *Union with Christ: The Way to Know and Enjoy God* (Colorado Springs, CO: David C Cook, 2016), Kindle edition.
12. Hudson Taylor, *Intimacy with Jesus: Understanding the Song of Solomon* (Littleton, CO: OMF International, 2000), 35–36. Song 2:16 in this quote is taken from the Holy Bible, New Living Translation, copyright © 1996, 2004, 2007, 2013, 2015 by Tyndale House Foundation. Used by permission of Tyndale House Publishers Inc., Carol Stream, Illinois 60188. All rights reserved.
13. Taylor, *Intimacy with Jesus*, 36.
14. Dee Brestin, "Worshiping Idols Without Knowing It: Interview with Dee Brestin," 11:58, *100 Huntley Street*, www.100huntley.com/watch?id=217363&title =worshiping-idols-without-knowing-it.

Chapter 7: I Sought the One My Soul Loves

1. Ellen F. Davis, *Proverbs, Ecclesiastes, and the Song of Songs* (Louisville, KY: Westminster John Knox, 2000), 256.
2. Davis, *Proverbs*, 261–2.
3. "Laura Story—Blessings," YouTube video, 4:59, posted by "laurastorymusicVEVO," October 29, 2013, www.youtube.com/watch?v=JKPeoPiK9XE&list=PL-Setdg6GIK Q6Lf48EBHYyBsqd0VUCcMJ.
4. "To Life: Vanessa's Wedding Surprise," YouTube video, 5:28, posted by "usnavi," September 8, 2010, www.youtube.com/watch?v=KgZ4ZTTfKO8&list=RDKgZ4 ZTTfKO8#t=0.

Chapter 8: An Oasis in the Wilderness

1. Mike Mason, *The Mystery of Marriage: As Iron Sharpens Iron* (Colorado Springs, CO: Multnomah, 2005), 125.
2. Ellen F. Davis, *Proverbs, Ecclesiastes, and the Song of Songs* (Louisville, KY: Westminster John Knox, 2000), 233.

Chapter 9: The Lukewarm Bride

1. For Tim Keller's sermons, see Gospel in Life, www.gospelinlife.com.
2. Chris Fabry, *War Room: Prayer Is a Valuable Lesson* (Carol Stream, IL: Tyndale, 2015), 85–87.
3. G. K. Beale and D. A. Carson, eds., *Commentary on the New Testament Use of the Old Testament* (Grand Rapids, MI: Baker Academic, 2007), 297.
4. Eric Metaxas, *Bonhoeffer: Pastor, Martyr, Prophet, Spy* (Nashville: Thomas Nelson, 2010), 165.
5. Stefan J. Bos, "African Man Turns to Christ Moments Before Beheading," *BosNewsLife*, April 23, 2015, www.bosnewslife.com/35141-african-man-turns-to -christ-moments-before-beheading.
6. "The 7 Churches of Revelation—Laodicea's History," YouTube video, 3:29, video of Cornerstone University president Joe Stowell's travels to modern Turkey, posted by "Day of Discovery," February 1, 2013, www.youtube.com/watch?v =oBJ5ElEilxQ.

Chapter 10: The Fairest of Ten Thousand

1. That is still true today. One report shows that 1 percent of sellers of these marketing plans make a profit; another shows 10 percent do. Many others lose their investment completely. Kate Shellnut, "Brand Evangelists," *Christianity Today*, December 2015, 37.
2. Ellen F. Davis, *Proverbs, Ecclesiastes, and the Song of Songs* (Louisville, KY: Westminster John Knox, 2000), 281–2.
3. Matthew Henry, *Matthew Henry's Commentary*, New Modern Version, vol. 4 (Peabody, MA: Hendrickson, 1991), 892.
4. "David Powlison—What Is Idolatry?" YouTube video, 3:15, posted by "CCEF PA," December 19, 2011, www.youtube.com/watch?v=hXUApsdmgT0.
5. C. S. Lewis, *Reflections on the Psalms* (New York: Harcourt, Brace & World, 1958), 90.
6. Lewis, *Reflections*, 93–94.
7. Daniel Philpott, quoted in Andrea Palpant Dilley, "The Surprising Discovery About Those Colonialist, Proselytizing Missionaries," *Christianity Today*, January 8, 2014, www.christianitytoday.com/ct/2014/january-february/world-missionaries -made.html.
8. To support this effective Christian ministry with prayer or finances, go to www .discipleshipunlimited.org.

9. "Jimmy Needham 'Clear the Stage' Official Lyric Video," YouTube video, 4:55, posted by "JimmyNeedhamOnline," March 29, 2002, www.youtube.com/watch?v =6smGew7dGto.

10. "Sara Groves—You Are the Sun (Official Pseudo Video)," YouTube video, 5:16, posted by "SaraGrovesVEVO," September 1, 2014, www.youtube.com/watch?v =1iqoEChUKGs.

Chapter 11: The Dancing Shulammite

1. Ellen F. Davis, *Proverbs, Ecclesiastes, and the Song of Songs* (Louisville, KY: Westminster John Knox, 2000), 290.

2. Mike Reeves, "The Love of Christ in the Song of Songs 1," Union Resources audio, 54:20, www.uniontheology.org/resources/bible/old-testament/the-love-of-christ-in -the-song-of-songs-1.

3. Davis, *Proverbs,* 290.

4. According to Ellen Davis, the Hebrew says this in Song 7:2; see Davis, *Proverbs,* 293.

5. Iain M. Duguid, *Song of Songs,* Reformed Expository Commentary (Phillipsburg, NJ: P&R, 2016), 131.

6. "Twila—Psalm 18," Vimeo video, 4:44, posted by "J.R. Brestin," July 12, 2016, https://vimeo.com/174968120.

7. "How Beautiful by Twila Paris (with Lyrics)," YouTube video, 4:40, posted by "Larry Hankins," October 9, 2015, www.youtube.com/watch?v=jVu5VZsCNOI.

Chapter 12: The Best Is Yet to Come

1. G. K. Chesterton, *Orthodoxy* (1908; repr., Chicago: Moody Classics, 2009), 82.

2. Martin Luther, *Martin Luther: Selections from His Writings,* ed. John Dillenberger (New York: Anchor Books, 1962), 61.

3. Philip Yancey, *The Jesus I Never Knew* (Grand Rapids, MI: Zondervan, 2002), 169.

4. Tim Keller, "The Freedom of Purity; The Sanctity of Sex (7th)" Gospel in Life audio, 40:35, June 12, 1994, www.gospelinlife.com/the-freedom-of-purity-the -sanctity-of-sex-7th-6332.

5. John Ortberg, foreword to Rankin Wilbourne, *Union with Christ: The Way to Know and Enjoy God* (Colorado Springs, CO: David C Cook, 2016), Kindle edition.

6. James M. Hamilton Jr., *Song of Songs: A Biblical-Theological, Allegorical, Christo- logical Interpretation* (Glasgow: UK, Christian Focus, 2015), 131.

7. Isaac Watts, "Joy to the World," 1719, public domain.

8. Win Couchman, "Beds I Have Known: A 72-Year-Old Story of Love and Devo- tion," *Just Between Us,* May 2016, 31. This revised version of the original article was sent to the author personally. Used by permission.

9. Richard Wurmbrand, *The Sweetest Song* (Bartlesville, OK: Living Sacrifice, 1988), 71.

10. Robert Robertson, "Come Thou Fount," 1758, public domain.

11. Charles Spurgeon, *Charles Spurgeon on the Song of Solomon: 64 Sermons to Ignite a Passion for Jesus!* (Christian Classics Treasury, 2013), Kindle edition.

12. "'I Must Leave You Now' by Danny Byram," YouTube video, 4:09, posted by "Danny Byram," February 20, 2014, www.youtube.com/watch?v=MOW _OvF1c8A.

Get-Acquainted Lesson

1. "Mike Reeves—Enjoying Christ Constantly," YouTube video, 13:31, posted by "WelcomeToTheSermon," May 2, 2013, www.youtube.com/watch?v=NRH _E2u5cGY.

Lesson-by-Lesson Leader Notes

1. "Mike Reeves—Enjoying Christ Constantly," YouTube video, 13:31, posted by "WelcomeToTheSermon," May 2, 2013, www.youtube.com/watch?v=NRH _E2u5cGY.

2. "Mike Reeves—Enjoying Christ Constantly."

3. Links to additional video material from Mike Reeves: set 1: "Union with Christ," messages 1–2, www.theologynetwork.org/the-holy-spirit-and-christian-living /union-with-christ-1-and-2.htm; set 2: "The Love of Christ in the Song of Songs," messages 1–4, www.theologynetwork.org/unquenchable-flame/the-reformation-in-britain/the-love-of-christ-in-song-of-songs.htm. In set 1, message 1, he doesn't get to the actual Song until the twenty-minute mark, though the beginning explains why we need the Song.

Printed in the United States
by Baker & Taylor Publisher Services